Recipes from Country Inns and Restaurants

Delia Smith

Photography by
Peter Knab

Recipes from Country Inns and Restaurants

London 1975

The Ebury Press

First published in Great Britain 1973
by Ebury Press
Chestergate House, Vauxhall Bridge Road,
London SW1V 1HF

Second impression 1975

Maps by E. and K. Morton

ISBN 0 85223 027 3

PUBLISHER'S NOTE, 1975

Since this book was first published in 1973,
some of the inns and restaurants may have
closed or changed hands.

Filmset and printed in Great Britain by
BAS Printers Limited, Wallop, Hampshire
and bound by
Webb Son & Co. Ltd, London and Ferndale

Contents

Introduction page 7
Inn Food in England 9

The West Country
The Lugger, *Portloe* 12
The Duke of York, *Iddesleigh* 14
The Highbullen, *Chittlehamholt* 16
The Horn of Plenty, *Gulworthy* 18
Ye Olde Masons Arms, *Branscombe* 20
The Priory, *Bath* 23
Pitt House, *Kingskerswell* 26
Bowlish House, *Shepton Mallet* 28
The Miners' Arms, *Priddy* 30

The Severn to the Thames
Harvey's, *Bristol* 34
The Bell Inn, *Ramsbury* 37
The Sign of the Angel, *Lacock* 38
The Elizabeth, *Oxford* 40
The Old Swan, *Minster Lovell* 42
The Dundas Arms, *Kintbury* 44
Thornbury Castle, *Thornbury* 46
Cleeveway House, *Bishop's Cleeve* 48
The Close, *Tetbury* 51

The South of England
Duck Inn, *Pett Bottom* 54
George and Dragon, *Fordwich* 56
Toastmaster's Inn, *Burham* 58
The Wife of Bath, *Wye* 60
Gravetye Manor, *Turner's Hill* 62
The Hungry Monk, *Jevington* 64
White Horse Inn, *Chilgrove* 66
The Old House, *Wickham* 68
Horton Inn, *Wimborne Minster* 70

Central England
The Hop Pole, *Bromyard* 74
The Pengethley, *near Ross-on-Wye* 76
The French Partridge, *Horton* 78
The Cottage in the Woods, *Malvern Wells* 80
The Elms, *Abberley* 82
The Hunter's Lodge, *Broadway* 84
Bells of Peover, *Lower Peover* 86
Churche's Mansion, *Nantwich* 88
Swan House, *Wilmcote* 90

East Anglia
Milton Ernest Hall, *Milton Ernest* 95
The Swan, *Stratford St Mary* 97
The Fox and Goose, *Fressingfield* 100
The Oysterage, *Orford* 102
The Pheasant Inn, *Keyston* 104
The De La Poste, *Swavesey* 106
The Pink Geranium, *Melbourn* 108
The Swan House, *Fowlmere* 110

The North of England
The Old Rectory, *Claughton* 114
The Dog and Partridge, *Chipping* 116
The Normandie, *Birtle* 118
The Old Rectory, *Haughton Green* 121
The Black Swan, *Helmsley* 122
The Old Manor House, *Knaresborough* 124
Pool Court, *Pool-in-Wharfedale* 126
The Star Inn, *Harome* 128

The Lake District
Leeming House, *Watermillock* 133
The Sharrow Bay, *Ullswater* 135
The Barbon Inn, *Barbon* 138
The Castle Dairy, *Kendal* 140
Tullythwaite House, *Underbarrow* 142
Three Shires Inn, *Little Langdale* 144
White Moss House, *Rydal Water* 146
The Miller Howe, *Windermere* 148

Basic Recipes for Reference 151

General Index 154
Classified Index 158

Acknowledgments

My grateful thanks to Caroline Liddell, for all the hard work she has put into testing many of these recipes and adjusting them to family-sized proportions. And for permission to reproduce the recipe for Priddy Oggy from Jane Grigson's book *Good Things* (Michael Joseph).

Introduction

If I were honest I would have to admit that this book began as a sheer self-indulgent exercise on my part. For someone like me who loves to cook, what could be more inspiring than to travel the length and breadth of England and meet and talk to the very best chefs in the country? I've never been one to get star-struck about footballers or filmstars; instead my ambition has been to get to know all the famous names in cooking, to talk to them, exchange ideas and, yes, collect recipes.

So that's exactly what I did. Just over a year ago I persuaded my husband (who didn't actually need much persuasion) to accompany me on a marathon tour which has preoccupied us for twelve months. With us came two close friends, Peter Knab and Diana Rowell (the photographic team) who, while I was closeted in the kitchen and my husband was investigating the historical backgrounds and architecture, braved the elements and climbed cliffs and mountains to produce the beautiful pictures in this book. I can assure you we loved every minute of it.

We set out to visit a cross-section of the whole range of country inns and restaurants, from the multi-starred and internationally famous to the more humble but homely sort of places. But one thing they *all* had in common was a complete dedication to producing good food, and it is my belief that the world – and indeed even most of England – is totally unaware of the tremendously high standard of cooking that is to be found up and down the country. And it saddens me to think of foreign visitors whose only taste of English cooking is in a motorway café. Even my own friends said, when we started, that I would never find enough recipes to fill a book. Well, we filled a book and could have done so twice over, I would add.

How does one set about choosing recipes from the enormous variety of tempting menus we were offered? In nearly all cases we left it to the cook or chef, with the only qualification that these recipes had to be suitable for cooking at home. Professionally trained chefs are sometimes fond of including *this* much demi-glace sauce, or *that* much fish fumet – which of course is just not feasible in a domestic kitchen.

We also gave up the idea of presenting a balanced menu from every establishment, because specialities are not always the simplest of recipes. However in virtually all cases we have taken a first course, a main course and a pudding course; this is simply to give the reader a cross-section of the sort of cooking which is done in a particular place. Please, therefore, do not assume that all three dishes are necessarily meant to be eaten at the same meal.

Finally we would like to say thank you to all the cooking people we have met from Cornwall to Cumberland, for their hospitality, for their patience (particularly when we have arrived at fraught moments), and above all for their help and kindness. I have always believed that people who cook are naturally nice people. And now I know it. To all of them this book is dedicated.

Delia Smith
September, 1973

Inn Food in England

Cooking in England owes a great deal to our country and coaching inns. As Dorothy Hartley points out in her book *Food In England*, many of the dishes 'that could be kept hot as well as "the cold stands", such as hams, pressed beefs, brawns and potted cheeses and dried biscuits, come from English inns. Also the more solid preserves, the lemon curds and almond fillings . . .'. And to these could be added local sauces and pickles, and many regional variations.

Traditionally it was required of an innkeeper not just to provide the traveller with a bed and a pot of ale, but to feed him as well. As travel became more widespread in the eighteenth century and coaching routes developed, many inns acquired a local (sometimes a national) reputation for their food, so that by the nineteenth century – when the English inn was still in its heyday – Mr Pickwick was able to progress across the countryside from one to another, and know well where he would be amply regaled with oysters or mutton pie or roast venison. Even later in the century, one of the characters in Disraeli's novel, *Tancred*, was much impressed by the food served him at a simple country inn:

> What mighty and iris-tinted rounds of beef! What vast and marble-veined ribs! What gelatinous veal pies! What colossal hams! Those are evidently prize cheeses! And how invigorating is the perfume of those various and variegated pickles!

Yet even as Disraeli wrote these words, a great tradition was dying. The stage coaches which had made the inns were giving way to the railways, as were the canals with their own intimate type of inn. The map of England was changing and the traveller had to put up with station buffets, or else he got where he wanted in time for lunch or dinner. Many notable coaching inns fell into disrepair, or became little more than alehouses for the local community, which had small need or desire to be fed at an inn.

The migration from the countryside, the shortages and rationing of two world wars, and the miseries of the Depression further combined to make the idea of 'eating out' a reckless indulgence for most people. Even with the advent of the motor car in this century, the new highways that were built rarely took any account of the inns that had stood for so long. New houses – now called public houses – were built to cater for the new, and faster, breed of traveller, but on the assumption that he had only time and inclination for a drink. It was an almost universal feature of these new red-brick establishments that no dining room was allowed for in the original plans. Meals, for those who could afford them, were now to be had in restaurants, and then almost exclusively in town centres. It is a sombre history, and accurately reflected in the decline of English cooking which continued progressively from the onset of the Industrial Revolution. But it is not the end of the story – as this book is intended to demonstrate.

For the fact is that since the last war we have witnessed a renaissance in England. Whatever the reasons – affluence, the effects of continental holidays, or an increased interest in and awareness of cooking on television and in magazines – cooking in this country has improved beyond all recognition. Most dramatic of all, perhaps, has been the revival of good food in restaurants, and that includes the country as well as London. Many delightful old inns now fill their dining rooms to capacity every night by adventurous and imaginative cooking. Even many pubs have begun to replace the one-time diet of crisps and salted peanuts by carefully cooked grills and snacks, with the encouragement of the breweries that own them (some enlightened companies, such as Allied Breweries, now have departments to help them).

That is not to say that all is well. There is infinite room for improvement, and some parts of the country are still gastronomic deserts, as we have discovered after travelling 10,000 miles round England in search of these recipes. Yet the signs are hopeful.

Because this is primarily a cookery book, it has not been possible to include very many inns which now provide first-rate food, whose strength lies not in the sophistication or culinary range of their meals, but in the quality of their ingredients and honesty of their cooking. But they deserve recognition. In the eighteenth and nineteenth centuries, the local inn always provided a ready market for local gardeners, fishermen and huntsmen (and doubtless, poachers as well). So it is a joy to find that some inns make a point of using local produce and, moreover, cooking it with respect as Mr and Mrs Dawson do with the pheasant from the local moors at the RED LION at Aramthwaite in Cumberland (Tetley); or as you'll find they do at the GEORGE AND DRAGON at Aldbrough on the Yorkshire coast with crab and lobster. And although there should be no excuse for any dining room to be offering soups made from packets (which, alas, we had on more than one occasion), many an inn could take a lesson in home-made soup from YE HORN'S INN up in Goosnargh, Lancashire (Tetley) or from Mrs Miller's Exford soup which we devoured at the CROWN at Exford on the north Devon moors (Watney). It was to be expected – or at least hoped – that country inns would be repositories of some of our traditional but largely forgotten regional recipes. So it proved, and some of them appear in later pages. But it was equally pleasing to come across our more straightforward native dishes cooked with consideration, like the brimming plateful of tripe and onions at the PARK at Chaddesden in Derbyshire (Ansell), the hot Cornish pasties at the LUGGER in Portloe, Cornwall (St Austell), and the massive Porterhouse steaks at the WITHIES INN, Compton in Surrey. In these days when the conventional answer to catering problems seems to be to install a 'steak' bar, it is almost a luxury to find all the meat at this Allied Breweries' inn grilled on charcoal.

From such places it was self-evidently not practical to seek recipes. And the same problem confronted us at the SHOULDER OF MUTTON in Fordham, Essex (Ind Coope), along with the four hundred and seventy-one different types of sandwich they have dreamed up there (for all we know it might be even more by now).

Another incidental pleasure has been to see how many of the ancient inns and houses have been restored to their former glory, both by interested individuals and by the breweries.

The saga of CHURCHE'S MANSION is told on another page, but similar wonders have been accomplished at West Bromwich, where the MANOR HOUSE (Ansell) has been rescued from dilapidation and now houses an enterprising restaurant. At the SWAN in Harleston, Norfolk (Adnams) the interior timbers are now seeing the light of day for the first time this century (and the menu is worthy of the new surroundings, too). Up in Bardsey, Yorkshire, at the BINGLEY ARMS (Tetley) an entire medieval chimneypiece concealing two priest's holes has been uncovered by diligent restoration. Equally genuine are the local quail, pheasant and York hams Mr Raeside serves here.

These are only a few of the agreeable places we came across on our travels: it would require another book to do them all justice. But, then, half the pleasure is discovering them for oneself. As Dr Johnson said: 'There is nothing which has yet been contrived by man, by which so much happiness is produced, as by a good tavern or inn'. Well, we enjoyed ourselves, anyway.

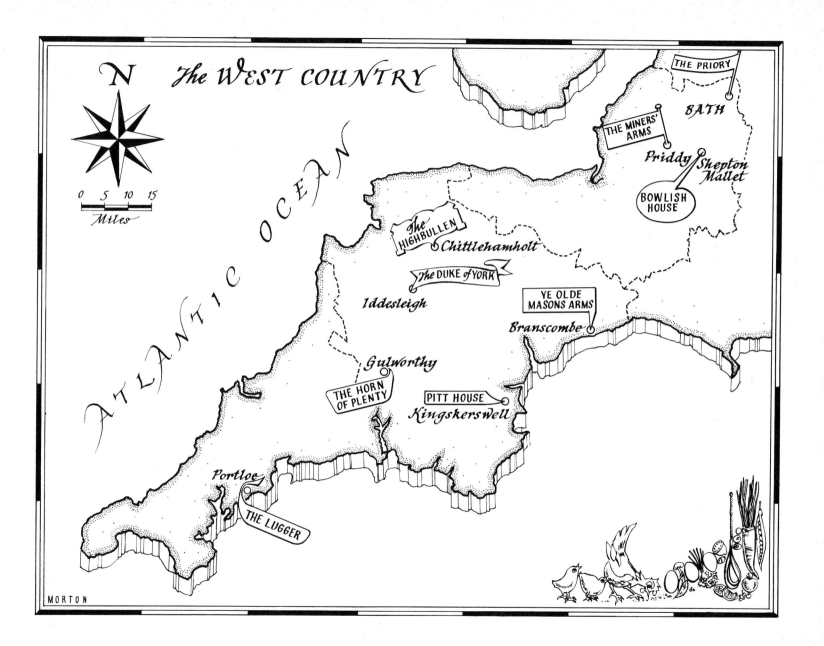

The Lugger

Portloe, Cornwall
Veryan 322

Portloe hides itself in one of those Cornish coves you read about in romantic stories of the Wreckers, but never seem to find when you look too hard. Drive down the tortuous cliff road, then walk on through the unspoiled village and down to the stone quay (follow the smell of the lobster pots) and when you can go no further there is The Lugger, the harbour water almost lapping against its walls. It has been an inn since the mid-seventeenth century – though the ships' timbers in the lounge clearly go back much further – and up in the bedrooms you can see where once the room partitions were hinged so that the fishermen could sling their hammocks.

Portloe today has but six working fishing boats but you can sit in the dining room (once the local boat-builder's shed) and imagine the great coal schooners coming in on the tide, or illicit French liquor and tobacco being off-loaded by moonlight. Oh yes, the Lugger was a smuggling inn all right – that's why it lost its licence in Victorian days, and one former landlord was even hanged for his pains. The inn has happily been back in business for the last twenty years and anyone who's tasted the Lugger's pasties or sea food will be glad it's still firmly rooted in the Cornish tradition.

Sea Food Mousse

½ lb of cooked white fish (free of bones and skin)
6 oz of cooked shellfish (prawns, scampi, scallops, etc)
½ oz of powdered gelatine
2 fl. oz of dry sherry
6 oz of crab meat (brown and white mixed)
4 fl. oz of thick mayonnaise

2 fl. oz of double cream
1 level tablespoon of tomato purée
The juice of ½ lemon
¼ level teaspoon of dried mixed herbs
Tasteless oil
Salt, freshly milled black pepper
Cucumber, lemon and watercress to garnish

12

First moisten a pad of kitchen paper with tasteless oil (e.g. groundnut) and use it to grease a 1-pint mould. Now pass the white fish and shellfish (not the crab) through the coarse blade of a mincer into a large bowl. The gelatine should be soaked in the sherry in a small basin for 5 minutes to soften, then placed over a saucepan of barely simmering water until the gelatine is completely dissolved and the mixture is absolutely transparent. Then remove it from the heat and allow it to cool slightly. Add the crab meat, mayonnaise and tomato purée to the minced fish, and beat well to mix everything thoroughly. Now stir in the strained gelatine mixture. Lightly beat the cream until it just begins to thicken, fold it into the mixture, taste, and add salt, freshly milled black pepper, lemon juice and herbs. Pack the mixture into the prepared mould and chill till firm. Turn out and garnish with paper thin slices of cucumber and lemon and sprigs of watercress. (*Serves 6*)

Beef Wellington

3 lb of well-trimmed fillet of beef (in one piece)
2 oz of liver pâté
1 medium onion (finely chopped)
¼ lb of mushrooms (finely chopped)
1 small green or red pepper (finely chopped)
1 clove of garlic
½ level teaspoon of dried mixed herbs
Seasoned flour, beef dripping
Salt, freshly milled black pepper
1 lb of shortcrust pastry
Beaten egg

Pre-heat the oven to 375°F (mark 5).

Coat the beef in seasoned flour, then quickly sauté it in very hot fat to seal. Place it in a roasting tin and part cook for 20 minutes. Now take it out of the oven, and allow it to cool. Meanwhile fry the chopped onion, mushrooms and pepper together, and while frying add a seasoning of salt, freshly milled pepper, crushed garlic and mixed herbs. The vegetables should be soft and almost cooked, then allowed to cool a little.

Roll out the pastry to a suitably sized oblong, spread the pâté over the middle of the pastry (to about the size of the meat) then spread half the vegetables over the pâté, and place the meat on top. Cover the top of the beef with the remaining vegetables, dampen the edges of the pastry, and fold the pastry round the beef, sealing well all round. Brush with beaten egg and make a few impressions across the top of the pastry with the back of a knife (these should only go about half-way through the thickness of the pastry). Place on a baking sheet, and bake in a hot oven (400°F (mark 6)) for ¾ to 1 hour, according to how you like your beef cooked. If the pastry starts to get too brown, cover it with a piece of foil. (*Serves 6*)

Rum and Blackcurrant Parfait

1 lb of blackcurrants (fresh or frozen)
½ a blackcurrant jelly
3 tablespoons of rum
3 oz of caster sugar
Cornish ice cream
Clotted cream

Make up the jelly according to the maker's instructions, and add about a third of the blackcurrants to it. Pour the mixture into 6 stemmed glasses and leave to set. Meanwhile soak the remaining blackcurrants in the rum and caster sugar. Just before serving, fill the remainder of the glasses with alternate layers of ice cream and blackcurrants, with a generous topping of clotted cream. Serve with biscuits. (*Serves 6*)

The Duke of York

Iddesleigh, Devon
Hatherleigh 253

Iddesleigh must be everyone's idea of an unspoilt English village. True, the forge has given way to a tractor engineer's, but otherwise it has changed only imperceptibly over the centuries. You approach it along alarmingly steep and narrow roads, high-banked on both sides. Then suddenly you are at the village green, flanked by gleaming white and thatched cottages, the inn, the post office, the school and the majestic church tower presiding benignly over, perhaps, a hundred souls. If it were not for the fame of the Duke of York, you would wonder what brought any traveller, ancient or modern, to these sleepy parts.

The Duke of York itself is a picture inn, thickly thatched and almost as thickly whitewashed. It was built in the thirteenth century and although civilisation has reached here, sophistication mercifully has not. Inside, it is a memorial to the simple, peaceful life, unadorned yet sociable. But there is nothing unsophisticated about Mrs Rafferty's famous cooking – unless it is the welcome absence of deep-freezing and the old-fashioned generosity with which it is served.

Baked Codling

1 lb of fresh codling or cod
½ onion (chopped very small)
½ clove of garlic (crushed)
2 rashers of bacon (rinded and chopped small)
2 oz of butter
1½ level tablespoons of flour
2 fl. oz of dry white wine
1 bay leaf
A few snipped chives
½ teaspoon of marjoram
2 tablespoons of breadcrumbs
Butter
Salt, freshly milled black pepper

Pre-heat the oven to 425°F (mark 7).

Poach the cod in salted water with a bay leaf added, then drain, reserving the cooking liquid. Remove the skin and bones etc., and flake the fish. In a thick-bottomed saucepan melt the butter and gently sauté the onion, garlic and bacon in it for about 8 minutes, then stir in the flour and add enough of the fish liquid to make a smooth thick sauce. Taste to check the seasoning, add salt and freshly milled black pepper, and then the white wine, chives and marjoram. Now stir in the flaked cod, and pour the mixture into 6 individual baking dishes, sprinkle with bread-crumbs, dot with a few flecks of butter, and brown in a hot oven for 15 minutes. (Serves 6)

Leg of Lamb Stuffed with Apricots

1 medium leg of lamb (ask the butcher to bone it for you, and trim most of the fat)

For the stuffing:
1 11-oz can of apricots
8 oz of fresh white breadcrumbs
1 medium onion (chopped very finely)
2 tablespoons of fresh chopped parsley
2 tablespoons of fresh chopped mint
½ level teaspoon of dried thyme
Salt, freshly milled black pepper

Pre-heat the oven to 350°F (mark 4).

Drain the apricots, reserving the juice, and chop them very small, then mix them with the breadcrumbs, onion and herbs. Add a good seasoning of salt and freshly milled black pepper, and bind the mixture with a little of the apricot juice. Spread the mixture inside the lamb (where the bone was), tie up with string into a neat roll, wrap in foil and bake slowly for about 45 minutes to the pound or according to how you like it. Remove the foil to brown the meat during the last 20 minutes of the cooking time. (Serves 6)

Banana and Ginger Meringue Cake

5 large egg whites
10 oz of caster sugar
1 tablespoon of vinegar
16 fl. oz of double cream
5 firm ripe bananas
6 large lumps of preserved ginger

Pre-heat the oven to 300°F (mark 2)

First prepare 2 baking sheets by wetting them and lining them with oiled greaseproof paper or non-stick parchment. Whisk the egg whites till they're stiff but not dry and form soft peaks when you lift the whisk. Now whisk in the sugar bit by bit (about 1 oz at a time) and when all the sugar is in, whisk in the vinegar. Now spoon the meringue into 2 circular shapes, one on each prepared tin, using a palette knife to help keep a round shape. Place the meringues in the oven, immediately turn the heat down to 275°F (mark 1), close the door and leave them there for an hour. Then turn the heat off and allow the meringues to cool and dry out inside the oven until quite cold. Before serving peel off the greaseproof paper and sandwich the 2 meringues together with whipped cream, the sliced bananas and finely chopped preserved ginger. (Serves 8 to 10)

The Highbullen

Chittlehamholt, Devon
Chittlehamholt 248

In autumn (and we discovered on a subsequent visit, in summer as well) the dawn mists roll along the Mole Valley so that disembodied trees appear to be floating on a cottonwool sea. And that is just one of the spectacular views the Highbullen (standing 600 feet up) offers at all times of the day. The house stands on land that in the 17th century belonged to the manor of Chittlehampton, but the present building is unashamedly Victorian, the spacious creation of William Moore of Exeter – who, local tradition has it, was careful never to quite finish the building, so that he could pay lower rates. However, for the past ten years, under Hugh and Pamela Neil, it has been a country-house hotel and anything but incomplete – with billiards room, swimming pool, croquet lawn and tennis court, even a special breakfast-room whose huge windows catch the first morning sun (if you can take your eyes off the freshest eggs you ever saw!).

All this, with Mr Neil's friendly hospitality and Mrs Neil's unforgettable cooking, make the Highbullen a haven of total relaxation. Her repertoire is large, and you would not exhaust it if you ate solidly for a month – but not to worry, the quality of it will bring you back again and again to Chittlehamholt (as it has us).

Armenian Mushrooms

¾ **lb of dark-gilled mushrooms (wiped and sliced)**
3 **rashers of bacon, streaky (chopped small)**
1 **clove of garlic (very finely chopped)**
2 **tablespoons of olive oil**
4 **fl. oz of red wine**
½ **red pepper (cut in thin strips)**
Freshly milled black pepper
1 **tablespoon of fresh chopped parsley**
4 **tablespoons of garlic mayonnaise (see page 151)**

In a large frying pan sauté the chopped bacon in olive oil until the fat begins to run, then add the mushrooms and garlic, and cook for a minute or two more, shaking the pan and stirring the mushrooms round. Then pour in the wine, turn the heat right up and let it bubble for about a minute to reduce a bit, then turn the heat down and cook for a further 4 minutes. Taste to check the seasoning, then turn into a serving dish, cool and chill. Serve garnished with thin strips of red pepper and fresh chopped parsley, with garlic mayonnaise. (*Serves 4*)

Noisettes of Lamb with Cucumber, Ham and Mint Sauce

12 prepared noisettes of lamb
2 tablespoons of oil
2 fl. oz of stock
2 fl. oz of red wine

For the sauce:
4 oz of lean ham (chopped small)
1 small cucumber (peeled and cut into matchstick strips)
1½ oz of butter
1 onion (finely chopped)
1 tablespoon of fresh chopped mint
4 tablespoons of thick cream
Salt, freshly milled black pepper

Blanch the cucumber by pouring boiling water over it, then drain thoroughly in a colander. Fry the noisettes in oil for 7 or 8 minutes, turning them once. In another pan melt the butter and fry the onion to soften (about 5 minutes), then stir in the ham,

cucumber and mint. Season well with salt and freshly milled black pepper, cook for a minute or two, then stir in the cream and keep warm over a very low heat. Don't let it boil. Remove the noisettes to a warm serving dish, pour the stock and wine into the pan and boil fiercely to make a little gravy. Pour this gravy over the noisettes and spoon the warm cucumber sauce all round the edge of the dish. Serve at once. (*Serves 4*)

Chinese Orange Cake

4 large eggs
4 oz of plain flour and
1 pinch of salt (sifted together)
6 oz of caster sugar
2 oranges
1 pint of double cream
1 level tablespoon of caster sugar for the cream
3 oz of crystalised ginger (finely chopped)
A few twists of orange peel
Extra preserved ginger for decoration

Pre-heat the oven to 375°F (mark 5).

First prepare 2 baking sheets by painting them lightly with oil and then dusting them with flour. Then mark each one with an 8-inch circle (using a plate as a guide). In a large mixing bowl whisk the eggs thoroughly with an electric mixer. Now gradually whisk in the sugar, a little at a time, and go on whisking until the mixture is really pale and thick. Carefully fold in the sifted flour, bit by bit, using a wooden spoon. Now divide a third of the mixture between the prepared tins and spread each one out evenly to form

an 8-inch circle. Bake these in the oven for about 8 minutes, remove, and when cool enough to handle transfer onto a wire cooling rack. Wash the baking sheets; oil and flour them again, and repeat the procedure twice more until you have 6 8-inch round sponges to form the gâteau. (Note: if you have 3 baking sheets, you will only need to do 2 lots, or you can cook them singly if you like – so long as you have 6 at the end.) Whip the cream till thick, adding the juice of 1 orange and the grated zest of 2, plus 1 level tablespoon of caster sugar. Assemble the cake together, filling each layer with whipped cream and a sprinkling of finely chopped ginger. Finish with a thick layer of cream on the top, and decorate with whole pieces of ginger and twists of orange peel. (*Serves 6*)

The Horn of Plenty

Gulworthy, Devon
Gunnislake 528

As you drive from Dartmoor Forest towards Bodmin Moor, just beyond Tavistock you will come across a sign-post pointing intriguingly to Chipshop. That was where once the lorry drivers of the nearby copper and arsenic mine exchanged their tokens or 'chips' for payment. Today it will take you to the Horn of Plenty, a fine nineteenth-century house commanding superb views over the River Tamar to the moors beyond. Formerly the captain of the mine lived here, who no doubt enjoyed its secluded position and would have been astounded now to discover it transformed into the mecca of food-lovers all over Britain.

So much has been written about Patrick and Sonia Stevenson's restaurant that there is little new to add. No one seems to have mentioned their impressive walled herb garden, but then all super-fluous descriptions are eclipsed by the superlative food and wine. And rightly so. They are both musicians – he an opera singer, she a violinist – but their artistry is nowadays directed towards the inner man rather than the spiritual, and when Mrs Stevenson applies her intuitive skills to some regional menu and Mr Stevenson his great knowledge to the attendant wines, the result is comparable to a great performance by Klemperer.

Potted Haddock

1 lb of smoked haddock (golden cutlets)
½ lb of unsalted butter (melted)
1 large pinch of Bolst curry powder (this is stronger than most blends)
2 or 3 tablespoons of lemon juice
Salt, freshly milled black pepper
4 level tablespoons of drained capers

Poach the fish, drain well and remove the skins. Place the fish in a blender or liquidiser with the melted butter and blend to a smooth paste. Turn the mixture out into a bowl, season with freshly milled black pepper, a little salt if it needs it, curry powder and enough lemon juice to your taste. Pack the mixture into 4 individual dishes, sprinkle with chopped capers, cover and chill till firm. Serve with toast. (*Serves 4*)

Canard en Casserole aux Poivres Verts

1 6-lb fresh duck with giblets
1½ pints of stock made from duck giblets
1 sprig of fresh thyme
1 level tablespoon of flour
1 level tablespoon of butter
3 tablespoons of Calvados
1½ level tablespoons of poivres verts (unripe peppercorns)
Salt, freshly milled black pepper

Pre-heat the oven to 350°F (mark 4).

Rub the duck inside and out with salt and freshly milled black pepper. Heat a deep metal casserole with the faintest touch of oil, and brown the duck in it on both sides over quite a fierce heat. Pour off any fat that escapes, return the pan to the heat, add the Calvados and allow it to bubble and reduce before adding the stock and a sprig of thyme. Bring to simmering point, then put a lid on the casserole and bake for 1½ hours. When the time is up, remove the duck, drain well and keep warm on a serving dish. Skim off all the surface fat from the casserole. Make a beurre manié by working the flour and butter together to form a stiff paste, then stir small pieces of the butter and flour mixture into the duck juices, bringing slowly to the boil and stirring constantly. Add the drained peppercorns, continue to simmer gently for a further 5 minutes, taste to check seasoning. Serve the duck with the sauce poured over. (*Serves 4*)

Lemon Crumble Cream

For the lemon cream:
¼ pint of milk
4 level tablespoons of caster sugar
Grated rind and juice of 4 lemons
1 level tablespoon of powdered gelatine
1 egg yolk
1¼ pints of double cream
4 large egg whites

For the topping:
5 wholemeal biscuits (crushed to crumbs)
1 oz of softened butter
2 level tablespoons of soft brown sugar

Prepare an 8-inch round cake tin by oiling it very lightly. Place the milk, sugar, grated

lemon rind, gelatine and egg yolk together in a blender or liquidiser, blend for half a minute at top speed, then pour the mixture into a small saucepan, and stir over a *very* gentle heat for 3 or 4 minutes until fairly hot but *not* boiling. Now return the mixture to the liquidiser and whizz round again, adding the lemon juice and ½ pint of the cream. When all is thoroughly blended, pour the mixture into a bowl, cover with foil and chill, stirring occasionally until the mixture is syrupy. Whip the remaining cream lightly until it just begins to thicken, then in another very large bowl whisk the egg whites till stiff and carefully fold them into the lemon mixture, followed by the cream. Pour the mixture into the cake tin, cover and chill until firm. Before serving, dip the cake tin for a moment in hot water, and turn the lemon cream over onto a plate. Mix the biscuit crumbs with the butter and sugar, sprinkle evenly over the top and serve. (*Serves 8*)

Ye Olde Masons Arms

Branscombe, Devon
Branscombe 300

As the narrow road through Branscombe dips and curves towards the sea, you are suddenly presented with a spectacular view below you of the Masons' Arms, almost devoured by clinging ivy. In its courtyard wooden benches are clustered round a curious thatched umbrella; the sign proclaims it to be Olde, and it certainly is – fourteenth century, much of it. Yet so ancient is Branscombe that this building is a comparative youngster. The village was once the Royal property of King Alfred, later passed to the Benedictines; the tower and nave of the parish church are pure Norman, and nearby Edgebarton Manor is believed to be the oldest inhabited house in England. Not only is it a perfectly preserved village, it's also an industrious one. Even if the smuggling trade has degenerated since the days of infamous Jack Rattenbury from Beer, fishing thrives (although the sea is a mile or so off now) and the traditional lace-making survives – Queen Alexandra's wedding dress was made here. The place is positively awash with clotted cream, and local bread is still baked in a sixteenth-century cottage oven. But perhaps most important for us, the art of good cooking too has been

preserved at the Masons' Arms by the Wilkinsons (and the Tudors who run it for them).

Crème Marie Louise

2 level tablespoons of chicken fat (or butter)
2 medium onions (finely chopped)
¾ lb of mushrooms (chopped)
2 level tablespoons of flour
1½ pints of chicken stock (see page 152)
Celery salt
6 parsley stalks
1 teaspoon of Worcestershire sauce
1 teaspoon of Soy sauce
Freshly milled black pepper

Melt the chicken fat in a large thick saucepan and gently fry the onions in it for 10 minutes or so without browning. Add the mushrooms and continue cooking slowly for another 5 minutes, then stir in the flour and gradually add the chicken stock, followed by a little celery salt and a few parsley stalks. Bring the soup to simmering point, put a lid on and simmer gently for 30 minutes. Now pass the soup through a fine sieve or liquidise, discarding the parsley stalks. Reheat gently, adding the Worcester and Soy sauces. Taste to check the seasoning and serve. (*Serves 4–6*)

Fillets of Lemon Sole with Shrimp Sauce

1½ lb of lemon sole fillets (plus bones, head, etc.)

For the stock:
Fish head and bones
A few parsley stalks
1 carrot (chopped)
1 onion (chopped)
1 stick of celery (chopped)
6 black peppercorns
1 bay leaf
Salt

For the sauce:
1½ oz of butter
1½ oz of flour
1 teaspoon of anchovy essence
1 tablespoon of lemon juice
4 fl. oz of double cream
¼ lb of peeled shrimps
3 tablespoons of dry white wine
A knob of butter
Salt, freshly milled black pepper

First make the stock by placing all the ingredients including the fish heads and bones in a saucepan with enough cold water to cover; bring to the boil and simmer for 20 minutes. Then strain and measure ½ pint ready for the sauce (the rest can be discarded). Butter a baking dish generously and place the fish fillets in it, folding each one in three. Season them lightly, then pour 3 tablespoons of wine over them and cover with a buttered piece of foil. Turn the oven on to 400°F (mark 6) and pre-heat, then start to make the sauce. Melt the butter in a thick saucepan, and stir in the flour till smooth. Cook for a minute or two, then start to beat in the ½ pint of fish stock, bit by bit, until you have a smooth thick sauce. Turn the heat very low and let the sauce cook for a few minutes. Then place the baking dish containing the fish on the highest shelf of the oven for 10 minutes to cook through. Now stir the anchovy essence and lemon juice into the sauce, followed by the shrimps. Stir, let them heat through, then stir in the cream and finally a knob of butter. Taste to check the seasoning. Keep the sauce warm, and when the fish is cooked pour the wine juices into the sauce. Stir them in, then pour the sauce over the fish, and serve. (*Serves 4*)

Lemon Griesetorte

4 oz of sugar
3 eggs (separated)
2 oz of semolina
½ oz of ground almonds
½ lemon (grated rind and juice)
4 tablespoons of lemon curd
¼ pint of whipped cream

Pre-heat the oven to 350°F (mark 4).

Put the egg yolks, sugar and lemon juice into a mixing bowl and beat until pale and thick. Then stir in the lemon rind, semolina and ground almonds, mixing evenly. Now whisk the egg whites until stiff and carefully fold them into the rest of the mixture. Pour the cake mixture into a prepared 7-inch round cake tin, place in the centre of the oven and bake for about 40 to 50 minutes, or until firm in the centre (if you have any doubt, insert a skewer in the middle and if it comes out dry and clean the cake is cooked). Allow the cake to cool for 10 minutes, then turn out onto a cooling tray, and when completely cool split in half. Spread both halves with lemon curd and whipped cream. Sandwich the halves together again, and serve cut in wedges. (*Serves 4–6*)

The Priory

Bath, Somerset
Bath 21887

Bath, as everyone knows, is redolent with history from the Romans to Beau Brummel. But one rather more recent piece of history, which for some of us could well rank alongside the opening of the Pump Room, is the advent of the Priory Hotel. For more than a hundred and thirty years this worthy Neo-Gothic building stood alongside its venerable cedar of Lebanon, falling short of its true vocation – until four years ago, when John and Thea Dupays transformed it from a private school into a private hotel. If, as they claim, they wandered into the business like innocents, you would never guess it from the international reputation the Priory has already built up.

It has been a marriage, one might say, of art, industry and imagination. The art is Mrs Dupays' – her vivid paintings light up the sitting room and her faultless taste gives every room a mood of its own. The industry is Mr Dupays', who took over the cooking two years ago when his wife was ill, and has acquired a formidable talent out of little more than a former knack for making chips. The imagination is in evidence every evening – whether in his adventurous main courses, or her subtle puddings and starters, like this delicate Sole St Germain.

Sole St Germain

6 fillets of sole
2 large cups of stale breadcrumbs (8 oz)
3 oz of grated Cheddar cheese
2 tablespoons of fresh chopped parsley
4 oz of melted butter
6 lemon quarters
Salt, freshly milled black pepper
A little extra melted butter

Pre-heat grill to its highest setting.

Mix the breadcrumbs, grated cheese and parsley with 4 oz of melted butter. Line the grill pan with foil, and paint the foil with melted butter. Lay the sole fillets on it and season them with salt and freshly milled black pepper, then cover them with the buttered breadcrumbs and pour over a little more melted butter. Place under the hot grill until the crumbs have turned a rich brown, and serve garnished with lemon. (*Serves 6*)

Mr Dupay's Game Pie

This, as you might guess, is not a recipe to be dashed off in a hurry – but it is a lot easier than it sounds, and so delicious and popular at the Priory that we felt it must be included in the book. As it's not really worth preparing a Game Pie for a small number of people, these quantities will serve 15 or 16 people and it is an ideal party dish, especially at Christmas time.

Part one:
6 pigeons
1 hare, quartered
3 lb scraps of venison (shin, belly etc)
1 pheasant
(none of the above need be high!)
¾ bottle of red wine
2 medium leeks
3 whole carrots
2 small turnips
2 sticks of celery
A clump of fresh parsley
1 sprig of fresh thyme
3 bay leaves
1 handful of raisins (stoned)
Flour
Butter and oil for frying
Salt, freshly milled black pepper

Part two:
3 carrots
2 turnips
3 leeks
4 sticks of celery
½ parsnip
1 heaped tablespoon of cornflour
2 large onions (sliced)
1 lb of large flat dark-gilled mushrooms

1 handful of raisins (stoned)
⅙ bottle of cheap port
1 tablespoon of redcurrant jelly
Salt, freshly milled black pepper

Plus:
1½ lb of puff pastry
Beaten egg

Method: part one
Season the pigeons, the quartered hare, venison and pheasant with salt and freshly milled black pepper. Dust them with flour, then fry until light brown on all sides in a mixture of butter and oil (you'll need two very large frying pans for this, and it's important not to overcrowd the pans but to carry out the whole operation by degrees). Transfer the browned meat to a huge (18-pint) sauce-pan, than add half the wine to the juices in one frying pan and the other half to the other pan, and reduce it slightly by fast boiling. Now pour the wine over the meat together with the prepared vegetables (left whole), the herbs and the raisins. Add a sprinkling of salt but not enough to season fully. Top up with

water – enough to almost cover the meat – bring to simmering point and simmer very gently for 45 minutes with the lid on. Allow everything to cool in the saucepan, then pick all the meat off the bones (putting it into a large bowl), replace all the bones and carcasses in the stock and boil that for an additional 30 minutes.

Method: part two
Chop the carrots, turnips, leeks (washed and split lengthways), celery and parsnip and place them in a saucepan with enough of the stock from the carcasses to cover them barely – you *must* use the stock, on no account use water. Simmer them gently until they are almost cooked, then pour them with the stock into the bowl of meat. Now strain and measure 1½ pints of the original stock into a saucepan (you can throw away the carcasses and old vegetables); mix a heaped tablespoon of cornflour till smooth with a little cold water. Pour it into the stock, simmer for 10 minutes and don't worry if it looks too thick as it will be diluted when you pour it over the meat and vegetables.
While the cornflour is simmering, fry the 2 large onions until they are just cooked, and lightly fry the large flat whole mushrooms (reserving the stalks for use later). When the cornflour stock is ready, pour it over the meat and vegetables, add the onions and mush-rooms, the port, redcurrant jelly and raisins and stir the whole lot together quite thorough-ly. Now for a final touch, which will add tremendously to the flavour and texture of the filling, quickly fry the mushroom stalks then liquidise them with a little stock and stir into the mixture. Taste to adjust the seasoning, then pour the mixture into two

large oval pie dishes. Top with puff pastry and decorate with leaves made from the left over bits of pastry. Glaze with a beaten egg and bake in a pre-heated oven (425°F (mark 7)) for 40 to 45 minutes until the pastry is cooked and golden brown.

(Note: if you don't have a large enough saucepan for cooking all the meat together, you can divide everything between two saucepans, or cook the meat in two separate lots, using the same stock for the second lot as for the first.) (*Serves 15 or 16*)

Priory Pudding

1½ lb of cooking apples (peeled and sliced)
1½ oz of butter
2 level teaspoons of cinnamon
4 oz of soft brown sugar
4 tablespoons of Calvados (or brandy)
1 tablespoon of water
3 large egg whites
6 oz of caster sugar

Pre-heat the oven to 325°F (mark 3).

Place the apples in a saucepan with the butter, cinnamon, sugar and Calvados. Add the water then simmer gently for 5 to 10 minutes, shaking the pan now and then. Meanwhile beat the egg whites until stiff, fold in half the caster sugar, beat again then fold in the other half. Put the simmered apple into a flan dish, cover with meringue, and bake in the oven for 35 to 45 minutes or until the meringue is nicely tinted. Serve hot or cold with lots of cream. (*Serves 4 or 6*)

Pitt House

Kingskerswell, Devon
Kingskerswell 3374

Since it was built in 1420, Pitt House has been many things. Tradition has it that it was originally the Dower House to the Manor of Kingskerswell (itself a ruin for more than two hundred years). The huge beam and weight in the garden suggest it was once a cider-pressing house – perhaps in the days when a stream still flowed through the kitchen to provide fresh water for the household. Later still its proximity to the old Brixham road turned it into a useful posting-stage where coaches changed horse while the passengers stoked up well for the next haul. If they were reluctant to press on, you can see why – particularly on a sunny day when you linger in the lovely garden, soaking up Devon tranquility and being amused by the infinitely good-humoured doves. The danger of this, as we discovered, is that you stay too long and miss a slice of Mrs Edwards' blackberry and apple pie. Still, the rest of her dedicated English cooking makes up for that, and there's consolation in Mr Edwards' fascinating wines.

Devilled Crab

1 lb of fresh crab meat (white and brown mixed)
3 oz of fresh white breadcrumbs
1 dessertspoon of anchovy sauce
1 level dessertspoon of French mustard
½ teaspoon of Tabasco sauce
1 tablespoon of brandy
4 tablespoons of double cream
2 level tablespoons of grated cheese
Freshly milled black pepper, salt
1 lemon cut into 6 wedges
Watercress

Pre-heat the oven to 450°F (mark 8).

In a large mixing bowl blend the first seven ingredients together carefully and thoroughly. Season with freshly milled black pepper, and taste to see if any salt is needed. Divide the mixture between 6 small individual heatproof dishes, sprinkle a little grated cheese over each one, and bake for 7 minutes. Serve immediately garnished with sprigs of water-cress and wedges of lemon. (*Serves 6*)

Jugged Hare

1 hare
Seasoned flour
Vinegar
2 tablespoons of oil
1 level tablespoon of butter
2 medium onions
3 medium carrots
3 sticks of celery
Bouquet garni (bay leaf, thyme, parsley stalks, crushed juniper berries tied together in muslin)
1 bottle of Burgundy
1½ pints of ham stock (or failing that, beef stock cube)
1 level teaspoon of flour
3 fl. oz of port
Redcurrant jelly
Salt and freshly milled black pepper

Joint the hare into 6 pieces, saving the blood to thicken the gravy (add a couple of drops of vinegar to the blood and keep it in an airtight container in the fridge). Wipe the joints of hare with kitchen paper, then coat them with seasoned flour. Now heat up the oil and butter in a large frying pan and fry the joints over a fairly high heat for 5 to 8 minutes, turning them frequently. Then remove them to a plate and leave them to cool. Meanwhile chop the onions, carrots and celery roughly, put them in a large strong watertight plastic bag, add the cooled hare joints and the bouquet garni (no pepper or salt is added at this stage), pour in the Burgundy and stock, seal the bag and leave to marinade for 1 or 2 days. (The reason for the plastic bag, Mrs Edwards says, is that it makes it easier to turn the joints over at regular intervals).

Pre-heat the oven to 300°F (mark 2). Place the contents of the bag in an earthenware or Pyrex casserole (avoid metal dishes for this), season, place uncovered in the oven and cook slowly for an hour. Then add the reserved blood of the hare mixed with a teaspoon of flour and cook for another hour or until the meat is tender and coming away from the bone. When cooked, add a large glass of port, taste to check the seasoning, and serve with redcurrant jelly. (*Serves 6*)

Meringue with Pitt House Chestnut Cream

1 round meringue base (see page 153)
8 oz of sweetened chestnut purée (tinned)
1 pint of double cream
2 tablespoons of rum
2 level tablespoons of sugar
6 whole marrons glacés
1 oz of chopped walnuts

Cream the sugar, marron purée and rum together in a mixing bowl, and beat in the cream a little at a time. Then whisk until the mixture is the consistency of whipped cream. Cover and chill. Just before serving, spoon the chestnut cream over the meringue base, decorate with the marrons glacés and chopped walnuts, and serve cut into wedges. (*Serves 6*)

Bowlish House

Shepton Mallet, Somerset
Shepton Mallet 2022

Shepton Mallet had its first moment of glory during the Duke of Monmouth's rebellion. Those were the days, in the seventeenth century, when the town had quite a reputation for its sheep (hence the name) and wool, and many fine cloth merchants' mansions testified to its prosperity. More recently it has been food and hospitality, not wool, which put this pleasant Somerset town back on the map – and Elaine Gardiner (yet another protégé of the Hole-in-the-Wall)

is one of the leaders of the new revolution.

When we first met her she was cooking wonders at Downside House. Since then she has moved to Bowlish House, a later but more spacious merchant's house. Shepton must be delighted she has stayed in the neighbourhood, and it can only be in the interests of good eating that now even more people can sample her homemade bread and three-course dinners cooked with such devotion and served – from soufflé to coffee – on dishes often designed and made by her husband, a potter by profession.

Aubergine Fritters with Tomato and Tarragon Sauce

1 lb of aubergines
2 level tablespoons of seasoned flour
Sunflower oil (for frying)

For the sauce:
2 oz of butter
1½ level tablespoons of flour
1 level tablespoon of tomato purée
1 16-oz tin of Italian tomatoes (liquidised or sieved)
2 tablespoons of white wine
1 level teaspoon of sugar
1 or 2 cloves of garlic (crushed)
2 tablespoons of fresh chopped tarragon (or 1 level tablespoon if dried)
Chopped parsley
Salt, freshly milled black pepper
Garlic croûtons (see page 153)

Prepare the aubergines by slicing them lengthways into slices about ¼ inch thick. Place them in a colander, sprinkle with salt and leave them for ¾ hour for all the bitter juice to come out. Meanwhile prepare the sauce: melt the butter in a thick saucepan, stir in the flour and tomato purée, then gradually add the sieved tomatoes, bit by bit, to make a smooth sauce. Now add 2 tablespoons of white wine, the sugar, salt, pepper, garlic and 2 tablespoons of tarragon, and let it simmer gently for 10 minutes. The aubergines should be dried thoroughly in kitchen paper or a clean cloth, dipped in seasoned flour, then (after the excess flour is shaken off), deep-fried till golden. Serve the aubergines scattered with garlic croûtons, with the sauce poured over and very liberally sprinkled with chopped parsley. (*Serves 4*)

Chicken in Soya and Ginger Sauce

1 4-lb chicken (cut into 4 pieces)
1 piece of fresh root ginger, about 1 inch in length (or 'Masterfoods' ginger in water)
6 fl. oz of thin soya sauce
1 clove of garlic (crushed)
1 level teaspoon of monosodium glutamate
Freshly milled black pepper
Vegetable oil for frying

Place the chicken joints side by side in a casserole. In a basin mix the soya sauce with the garlic and the ginger (which should be cut in wafer-thin slices), and add the monosodium glutamate. Season the chicken with freshly milled black pepper (but *no* salt, because it's already in the soya sauce). Pour the mixture over the chicken and leave in a cool place to marinade for 2 to 3 hours.

Pre-heat the oven to 350°F (mark 4), then remove the chicken joints from the marinade and fry them in hot vegetable oil until the skin is crisp. Then pour the marinade back over, and cook for a further minute or two. Now transfer everything back into the casserole, put on a lid and cook in the lower part of the oven for 1 hour. Serve with rice and a crisp green salad. (*Serves 4*)

Caramelised Peaches and Pears

2 firm ripe peaches (peeled and cut in bite-sized pieces)
2 firm ripe pears (prepared as the peaches)
¼ pint of double cream and
1 level tablespoon of caster sugar, whipped together until thick
4 or 5 level tablespoons of good quality demerara sugar

Arrange the fruit in a shallow fireproof dish and cover with sweetened cream, smoothing this down with a spatula so that the fruit is completely covered. Sprinkle thickly with demerara sugar, then place the dish in the freezing compartment of the refrigerator for 30 minutes, or until the cream is solid. Pre-heat the grill until very hot and put the dish underneath until the sugar starts to caramelise. Serve at once. (*Serves 4*)

The Miners' Arms

Priddy, Somerset
Priddy 217

The miners in question, of course, were lead miners. They say you can hardly put a spade in the ground hereabouts without hitting history, and lead was mined long before the Romans came to dig it up for their plumbing in Bath. This inn, on its windswept Mendip ridge, was built to accommodate the miners in the late seventeenth century – and a rough lot they were, to judge by the marks that can still be seen on the lounge floor, said to be evidence of a feud from those violent days. The mines began to peter out in the nineteenth century; but Priddy, once a bustling centre, has clung on to one piece of history – its Holy Legend, which says that when Joseph of Arimathaea made one of his journeys to Britain to look for lead, he brought the young Jesus with him, which, you have to admit, is one up on Glastonbury.

Today the lead-workings around Priddy have been covered by the Forestry Commission, and the Miners' Arms has taken on a new lease of life under Paul Leyton and his wife. Mr Leyton, who was formerly in charge of the construction of Britain's first space rocket, has now constructed a world-famous menu of local delicacies such as Priddyoister, Quenelles of Trout (which we would have offered as a first course, but instead recommend that you buy direct from Mr Leyton – see below) and Priddy Pâté. The back garden is amok with Mendip Snails, and every autumn he smokes his own pork in the ancient fireplace of the inn. For those unable to make the détour to Priddy from the Cheddar Gorge, Mr Leyton's engineering has brought many of his famous dishes within reach of the whole world with his own special frozen mail-order service (write to him for a brochure).

Priddy Oggy

Pork tenderloin stuffed with a cheese, herb and egg paste, wrapped with smoked pork and encased in cheese-flavoured pastry.

For the cheese pastry:
½ lb of plain flour
1 oz of butter
1 oz of lard
1 small egg yolk
3 ½ oz of mature Cheddar (grated)
2 ½ tablespoons of water
A pinch of salt

Meat:
1 pork tenderloin, weighing approx 1¼ lb
1 oz (at least) of very thinly sliced smoked pork or smoked bacon

For the stuffing:
3 oz of mature Cheddar (grated)
A sprig of parsley (chopped)
A pinch of salt
8 drops of Tabasco (or cayenne pepper)
1 large egg

Lard for frying

Make the pastry first. Mix all the ingredients (except the flour) in a bowl – it helps if you warm the butter and lard slightly. Cool the mixture in the refrigerator until firm, then sift the flour and rub the cooled mixture in roughly. Take about 3 to 4 oz of this crumble pastry and roll it two or three times into a ½-inch slab. Repeat, placing each slab upon the other: moisten the top of the pile before putting another slab of pastry on it. Press down firmly and cut into several 3- or 4-oz lumps. Repeat the rolling process twice more. Leave for 30 minutes in a cold place. Cut into 8 pieces, and squeeze each one into a sausage shape, and roll out to measure 4 to 6 inches. Leave to rest for an hour.
Trim the tenderloin of fat and skin, slice it lengthways into equal halves, and beat them gently until they are ¼ inch (or very little more) thick. Cut the smoked pork or ham into 8 strips. Now make the cheese stuffing. Beat the egg and put half of it aside. Mix in the cheese, parsley, salt and Tabasco with half the egg. Spread evenly over the two cut sides of tenderloin. Roll up each piece, press down firmly and leave in the icebox of the refrigerator to harden.

To assemble the oggies, cut each roll of tenderloin into 4 pieces. Wrap each round with a strip of smoked pork or ham. Lay each little parcel in the middle of a piece of pastry (which should be moistened round the edge with milk). Bring the pastry up and over the pork, pressing the two edges together in a scalloped crest as in a Cornish pasty. Press down to flatten the base and trim where necessary. Brush with the remaining egg and bake for 10 minutes at 325–350°F (mark 3–4), until the pastry begins to brown. Finish in deep fat, or fry in lard, turning the oggies over until they are golden brown. Before cooking they can be stored in the refrigerator for 3 days or in a deep freeze for 3 months (in the latter case, give them 15 to 20 minutes in the oven before frying). (*Serves 8*)

Lemon Syllabub

1 large lemon (rind and juice)
2 tablespoons of brandy
3 tablespoons of white wine
1 tablespoon of sherry
2 oz of granulated sugar
1 small coffeespoon of freshly grated nutmeg
1 pint of double cream

Place all the ingredients except the cream and nutmeg in a basin, leave mixture for a minimum of 2 hours, but as long as possible to let the sugar dissolve, then strain it into another basin and gradually whip in the double cream bit by bit (a balloon whisk is best for this). When all the cream is in and the mixture just holds its shape, add the grated nutmeg. Pour into individual glasses and chill until ready to serve. Syllabub improves with keeping so it's really better made the day before. (*Serves 8*)

Orange Conserve

6 thin-skinned oranges
2 lb granulated sugar
Water
1 fl. oz of orange Curaçao
1 fl. oz of brandy

Scrub the oranges thoroughly with a stiff brush, then place them in a pressure cooker with enough cold water to make them *just* float. Cover and bring the pressure up to 15 lb per square inch. Cook for exactly 3 minutes, then immediately remove pressure cooker from heat and leave it to cool; keep it at room temperature for 12 hours or overnight. Next day remove the oranges from the water, then using your sharpest knife, slice them as thinly as possible, discarding all the pips and the first and last slices of each orange (because they're mostly peel). Pour the poaching water into a large saucepan, add the granulated sugar, then bring very slowly to the boil, stirring all the time until the mixture thickens and reaches 213°F on a cooking thermometer. Add the slices of orange and continue to boil gently until the thermometer shows 214°F, at which point the syrup will be tacky when tested by dripping onto a cold plate. Cool until below 150°F but still warm, then stir in the spirits and store in covered jars in a cool place.

Oranges preserved in this way will keep indefinitely, and are best served with whipped cream flavoured with a little orange Curaçao. This amount will provide approximately 12–14 servings.

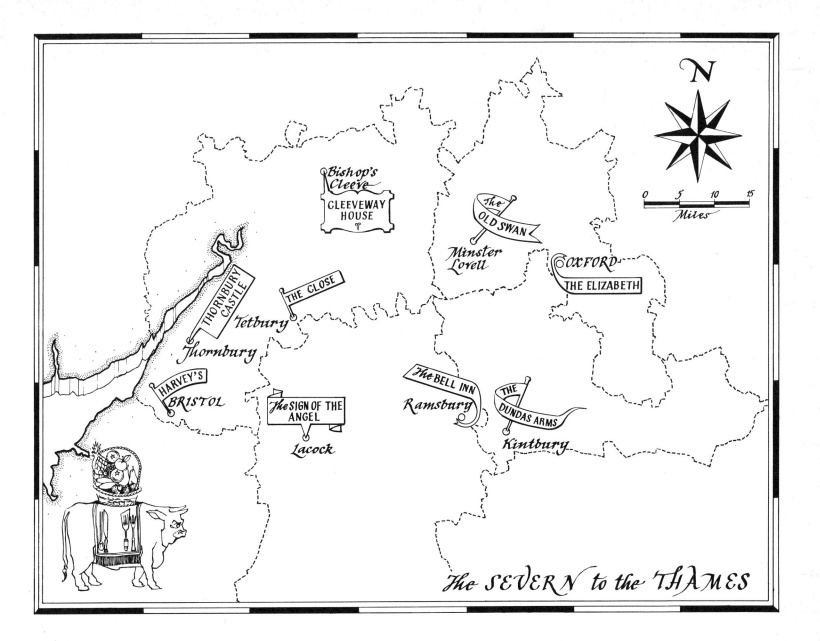

The SEVERN to the THAMES

Harvey's

Bristol
Bristol 27665

You would never guess, standing in Bristol's busy city centre, that such a maze of tunnels and cellars ran beneath the pavements. The entrance to them, behind the Hippodrome, marks the site of the fifteenth-century Gaunt's House (sadly destroyed in a 1940 air-raid). The cellars themselves date back even further, to 1140, when they served as store-rooms for the monastery of St Augustine (whose church is now Bristol Cathedral). In the thirteenth century they became part of the Hospital of the Gaunts, dedicated to the poor and sick but destined itself to waste away after the Dissolution. Two hundred and fifty years after a new and magnificent house had been built on the spot, there came to live there William Perry, a budding wine merchant who founded the business now known as Harvey's and whose cellars were soon crammed with the cargoes of Bristol ships bound from Jerez and Oporto.

Today the cellars house only a fraction of Harvey's stock, but what there is is breathtaking: claret laid down during the Crimean War and ports grown while Wellington was still tramping the Peninsula. In another part of the cellars, cleaner of course and warmer, there is a restaurant whose wine list, understandably, is considered to be the best in the country. The menu, too, is not forgetful of its surroundings and always offers some speciality based on Madeira or sherry. Elsewhere below ground is Harvey's wine museum – well worth a visit, preferably before rather than after your generous meal.

Fonds d'Artichauts Brimont

4 globe artichokes
1 tablespoon of lemon juice
4 oz of lobster meat (or crab or prawns)
½ lemon

For the sauce:
⅛ pint of mayonnaise (see page 151)
1 level dessertspoon of tomato purée
1 teaspoon of brandy
1 pinch of cayenne pepper

Break off the stalks from the artichokes, trim the points of the leaves with scissors and cut about ½ inch off altogether. Place them in boiling salted water with the lemon juice added, and boil for 20 to 25 minutes, or until the bases are tender when tested with a skewer and the leaves pull off easily. Drain the artichokes upside-down in a colander, and when cool enough to handle, pull out the leaves and remove the chokes, leaving the fonds (bottoms) intact. Now rub the fonds gently with the half lemon (to prevent them from discolouring). Mix all the sauce ingredients. Place each fond in the centre of a serving dish, arrange the leaves round the edges for decoration, mix the flaked lobster with the sauce and spoon it into the centre of each fond. Garnish with artichoke leaves cut into thin slices. (*Serves 4*)

Noisettes de Veau Bristol

1½ lb of small fillets of veal, beaten out flat (taken from the upper part of the loin)
½ lb of button mushrooms (sliced thinly)
4 fl. oz of Madeira
2 oz (approx) of butter
Salt, freshly milled black pepper
A few sprigs of watercress
Savoury rice (see Pilaff, page 71, but omit currants and nuts, if preferred)

In a large heavy frying pan sauté the thinly sliced mushrooms in some butter for about 5 or 6 minutes (shaking the pan to turn them over now and then). Using a slotted spoon,

remove the mushrooms to a warmed serving dish and keep warm. Now add the rest of the butter to the pan and gently sauté the thin slices of veal, which should be seasoned with salt and freshly milled black pepper. When the veal is cooked on both sides, arrange it on top of the mushrooms. Pour the Madeira into the pan and let it bubble and reduce a bit, stirring it into the pan juices. Then pour over the veal, garnish with sprigs of water-

cress, arrange some savoury rice all round the dish in a border, and serve. (*Serves 4*)

Chocolate Mousse Harvey

6 oz of plain chocolate
6 small eggs (separated)
1 level teaspoon of instant coffee powder
2 tablespoons of brandy
3 oz of caster sugar

Place the broken up chocolate squares in a basin and fit the basin over a saucepan of barely simmering water. Dissolve the coffee powder in a little hot water and add it to the chocolate. Then stir now and then until the chocolate has melted completely and is free of any lumps. Now remove the melted chocolate from the heat and beat in the egg yolks and the brandy till smooth and glossy. Whisk the egg whites until stiff, then gradually beat in the caster sugar and continue whisking. Fold about a quarter of the egg white mixture into the chocolate mixture to loosen the consistency, then gently fold in the remainder. Pour the mixture into 4 individual glasses or dishes, and chill thoroughly until firm. (*Serves 4*)

The Bell Inn

Ramsbury, Wiltshire
Ramsbury 230

Once there was a monastery in Ramsbury and, long before Salisbury raised its spire in the thirteenth century, it was the cathedral 'city' of the neighbourhood (until the bishops quit, complaining, it's rumoured, of the rheumatism). Possibly the Bell, in its earlier foundation, had some ecclesiastical connections, but it looks today what it has been for centuries – a rural coaching inn, complete with welcoming fireplaces and misguided, though no doubt well intentioned Victorian additions.

Like his surroundings Brian O'Malley has a monastic past. He was for a number of years a Trappist, and talking to him now you can surely detect a genuinely spiritual approach to cooking. Romantic would perhaps be a better description: he finds his inspiration, he says, among forests and in the soil. And that is no idle chat, for when it comes to the unmystical business of cooking, his menus are truly original. If English cooking is ever to regain its former eighteenth-century glory it will be through men like Mr O'Malley. To him, the jibe that England has only one sauce is a personal reproach, and one that wouldn't stand up for a moment at the Bell.

Soused Salmon

4 small salmon steaks (approx ¾ inch thick)
4 fl. oz of dry white wine
1 dessertspoon of white wine vinegar
4 thinly sliced apple rings
4 thinly sliced onion rings
4 thin slices of lemon (with peel)
2 tablespoons of capers (drained)
Salt, freshly milled black pepper

Place the salmon steaks side by side in a large frying pan, season them with salt and freshly milled black pepper, then add all the other ingredients. Cover the pan and simmer gently for 5 or 10 minutes, then transfer everything to a serving dish. Allow to get quite cold, then cover and chill until ready to serve as a first course. (*Serves 4*)

Sussex Steak

2 lb of rump steak (trimmed and cut into 4)
Flour
6 tablespoons of port
6 tablespoons of stout
1 tablespoon of mushroom ketchup
1 teaspoon of sherry
1 level dessertspoon of tomato purée
1 onion (chopped small)
¼ lb of dark-gilled mushrooms with stalks, field mushrooms if possible (chopped)
Beef dripping
Salt and freshly milled black pepper

Pre-heat the oven to 300°F (mark 2).

In a large frying pan heat some dripping or butter and gently fry the chopped onion and mushrooms for 5 minutes or so. Dry the steaks in some kitchen paper and dust them with flour, then add them to the onion and mushrooms. Fry them nicely brown on both sides. Now stir in the tomato purée and mushroom ketchup, add the stout, port and sherry and a seasoning of salt and freshly milled black pepper, then transfer everything into a casserole. Cover and bake slowly in the oven for 3 hours, by which time it will emerge beautifully tender, with the gravy rich, brown and well flavoured. (*Serves 4*)

Wiltshire Cream

4 Huntley and Palmers sponge fingers
2 tablespoons of sweet sherry
2 egg yolks
1 egg white
1 oz of caster sugar
¼ pint of double cream (lightly whipped)

Break up the sponge fingers and arrange them in four small stemmed glasses, then moisten them with half the sherry. Whisk the egg yolks and sugar till pale and creamy, add the rest of the sherry to the egg yolk mixture, then fold in first the lightly whipped cream followed by the stiffly beaten egg white. Pour the mixture into the glasses, chill and serve with more sponge fingers to go with it. (*Serves 4*)

The Sign of the Angel

Lacock, Wiltshire
Lacock 230

You may not notice it at first, because the village of Lacock has a rare and hypnotic beauty, but there are no television aerials or telephone wires anywhere to be seen. Under the custody of the National Trust they have all been tucked away or buried underground. As nearly as is humanly possible, Lacock must look exactly as it did when Talbot exposed the first photographic negative here in the early years of the last century — indeed, as it looked long before that. For the Sign of the Angel is a mediaeval building (records show that in 1485 its occupants were fined 'for allowing singers in the house after 9 o'clock') and it is by no means the oldest building.

Even the best traditions of innkeeping seem to have been preserved at the Angel. Nothing is too much trouble for the Levis family who now run it — not even a rather recalcitrant fire-place which is a joy when alight, but doesn't give in without a struggle. Dining without candlelight would be unthinkable here, just as a French menu would be. No fear of that: Mrs Levis' cooking is English to the core, generous, comforting and as unspoiled as Lacock itself.

38

Lacock Liver Pâté

1½ lb of duck livers
½ lb of pig liver
1 lb of belly pork
¾ lb of thin streaky bacon
1 onion (finely chopped)
1 clove of garlic (crushed)
3 eggs (beaten)
2 tablespoons of brandy
1 teaspoon of oregano
4 whole cloves
2 oz of butter
2 oz of flour
¼ pint of milk
3 bay leaves
Salt, freshly milled black pepper

Pre-heat the oven to 325°F (mark 3).

Take a large chopping board and a sharp knife and cut the liver and pork into very small pieces (for this pâté the meat should *not* be minced). Then in a large mixing bowl mix the meats with the eggs, brandy, onion, salt, freshly milled black pepper and the rest of the seasonings (the cloves should be crushed finely in a pestle and mortar). Melt the butter in a small saucepan, stir in the flour and gradually add the ¼ pint of milk, stirring vigorously to make a thick sauce (panada). Then stir this thoroughly into the meat mixture. Line a 2½- or 3-pint oval pie dish or terrine with thin slices of streaky bacon. Pour the meat mixture into the dish, cover with foil and place in a roasting tin half filled with water. Then bake for about 3 hours. (*Serves 12*)

Traditional Roast Duck with Sage and Onion

1 duck approx. 5½ to 6-lb (with giblets)
8 oz of fresh white breadcrumbs
2 oz of dripping
Salt, freshly milled black pepper
1 oz of fresh sage leaves (finely chopped)
1 lb of onions
3 level tablespoons of flour seasoned with salt

For gravy:
Parsley
Carrot
2 level tablespoons of flour
Grated orange rind

Pre-heat the oven to 400°F (mark 6).

Peel and chop the onions and boil them in 1 pint of water for about 20 minutes, then drain and reserve the onion water. In a mixing bowl combine the breadcrumbs and sage with the dripping and a good seasoning of salt and freshly milled black pepper. Then pour in the drained onion, mix again and pack the mixture inside the duck, tucking the neck flaps underneath and securing with a small skewer. Rub the duck well with salt and flour, place it on a grid in a dry baking tin, and bake in a hot oven for 1½ to 2 hours. Meanwhile cook the giblets in the onion water (with a bunch of parsley and a carrot). When the duck is cooked, remove it onto a warmed serving dish and keep warm. Pour off all the surplus fat from the roasting tin, then over a gentle heat stir 2 tablespoons of flour into the duck juices, add a small grating of orange rind and allow the mixture to brown. Then gradually stir in the strained giblet stock to make a rich gravy. Serve the duck with the gravy and some apple sauce to go with it. (*Serves 4*)

Apple and Almond Pudding

1 lb of cooking apples
2 oz of soft brown sugar
4 oz of ground almonds
4 oz of butter (room temperature)
4 oz of caster sugar
2 eggs (beaten)

Pre-heat the oven to 350°F (mark 4).

Stew the apples till soft with the brown sugar and approximately 1 tablespoon of water, then arrange them in the bottom of a buttered pie dish. In a mixing bowl cream the butter and sugar until pale, light and fluffy, then beat in the eggs a little at a time. When they're all in fold in the ground almonds. Spread this mixture over the apples, making the surface even with the back of a spoon, and bake in the oven for exactly 1 hour. This pudding can be served warm or cold, and will keep in the refrigerator for up to a week. (*Serves 4 or 6*)

The Elizabeth

Oxford
Oxford 42230

For all that the building was originally part of the old Bishop's Palace, the main dining room at the Elizabeth has the comfortable air of an undergraduate's college room. And that's really what it once was, because recently a former occupant returned to visit his old quarters and stayed to dinner. The view from the window is straight out of *Zuleika Dobson*: to your left the silhouette of Tom Tower, in front of you the path through the Meadows to the river. Next door to you could well be a philosopher or philologist, but if there is anything academic about the cooking it is only its accuracy and quality.

Antonio Lopez came to Oxford to learn to speak English. That was in the days when Kenneth Bell (see Thornbury Castle) was making the Elizabeth famous; and instead of returning to Spain as intended, Mr Lopez remained here to cook, and eventually to take over. To have maintained the glorious reputation of the Elizabeth would qualify him for first-class honours, and there are countless Oxford palates which will testify Mr Lopez has done just that, and more. And *de gustibus non disputandum*, as they say in the senior common rooms.

Quiche aux Crevettes

For the pastry:
4 oz of plain flour
2 oz of butter
1 egg
Salt

For the filling:
2 oz of prepared washed leeks (chopped)
2 oz of butter
2 eggs
1 teaspoon of fresh chopped parsley
4 oz of soft cream cheese
4 oz of prawns
¼ pint of fresh double cream
½ level teaspoon of salt
A little freshly grated nutmeg
A pinch of cayenne
1 clove of garlic (crushed)
¼ pint of fish stock – see page 152 – (boiled in an uncovered saucepan till reduced to 2 tablespoons)

Make the pastry ahead of time (in the morning). Rub the butter into the sifted flour and salt, using your fingertips, and add a beaten egg to make a soft pliable dough – if the pastry seems a little dry add a drop or two of water. Wrap the pastry in foil and leave it in the fridge till needed.

To make the quiche, first roll out the pastry to line a buttered 8- or 9-inch round baking tin. Pre-heat the oven to 375°F (mark 5), and put a flat baking sheet in to pre-heat as well. For the filling, sauté the leeks in the butter until pale golden, then transfer them to the pastry case, using a draining spoon. In a basin mash the cream cheese with a fork and gradually combine it with the beaten eggs, cream and concentrated fish stock, and beat till smooth. Add the prawns, parsley, crushed garlic and the rest of the seasonings. Pour this mixture into the prepared pastry case, place it on the baking sheet and bake for 40 to 45 minutes until it has risen slightly and turned a beautiful golden brown. The quiche is cooked when it is firm to touch in the centre. Serve immediately straight from the oven. (*Serves 4 to 6*)

Lamb Chilindron

2 lb of boned lamb, cut from the shoulder
1 large onion (roughly chopped)
2 large fat cloves of garlic (crushed)
¾ lb of tomatoes (peeled and chopped)
½ lb of red peppers (chopped) *or*
    14 oz can, drained and chopped
4 oz of cured ham (chopped)
2 tablespoons of olive oil
Salt, freshly milled black pepper

Cut the lamb into large cubes approximately 2 inches square. Heat the oil in a flameproof casserole, and brown the meat till golden on all sides. Now add the onion, garlic and ham, and continue to cook until the onion has softened. Then add the tomatoes and red peppers, and season with salt and freshly milled black pepper (remembering there will be *some* salt in the ham). Put a lid on and simmer very gently with the heat very low for about 1 to 1½ hours or until the meat is tender (during the cooking time, give the meat a couple of stirs). Serve with potatoes and any vegetable in season. (*Serves 4*)

Crème Brûlée

1 pint of fresh double cream
1 level tablespoon of white sugar
1 vanilla pod
6 egg yolks
6 level tablespoons of soft brown sugar

In a saucepan boil the pint of double cream together with the vanilla pod and white sugar, then remove the vanilla pod from the mixture. Now place the separated egg yolks in the top part of a double saucepan (filling the bottom with water), then over a low heat add the cream and cook until it has thickened considerably. When the custard is made, pour it into 6 individual earthenware or fireproof bowls, and let it settle for several hours – or overnight – in the refrigerator. Then put a tablespoon of soft brown sugar on top of each earthenware bowl and smooth. Pre-heat the grill to very hot, then burn the sugar under the grill. Keep in the refrigerator until required, bearing in mind that once the sugar is added this will keep for a few hours only. (*Serves 6*)

The Old Swan

Minster Lovell, Oxfordshire
Asthall Leigh 614

As the River Windrush runs out of the Cotswold hills and before it joins the Thames, it flows peacefully past the eleventh-century priory of Minster Lovell (now a ruin, but an exceedingly pretty one). Nearby stands the Old Swan, as it has stood here for five hundred years (and parts of it for a great deal longer), with wooden benches lining the mature stone walls in summer, and whole oak logs burning in the voluminous fireplaces in winter. In the days when drovers en route to London laid out their rush sleeping mats in front of them (leaving their charges down the road on what is still called Pound Ground), this inn was called the White Swan. But now she has grown old, and the drivers are more likely to be the better-heeled undergraduates from Oxford.

This Ind Coope inn gained a reputation for fine food years ago under the Cleggs (who still have an interest in it), but it has lost nothing under Mr Buckley's reign. The chef has presided over the kitchens for eleven years, and the head waiter over the dining room for no less than thirty-two years (why, only sixty-odd years ago it was still a brew house). But it's that sort of place – where time obligingly slows down.

42

Taramasalata with Cream Cheese

½ lb of cream cheese
3 oz of smoked cod's roe (weighed after the skin is removed)
½ onion (very finely chopped)
2 cloves of garlic (crushed)
2 tablespoons of lemon juice
1½ tablespoons of fresh chopped parsley
Freshly milled black pepper

Pound the cream cheese together with the cod's roe (either in a pestle and mortar or with a wooden spoon). Add the rest of the ingredients, blend evenly, then press the mixture through a fine sieve. Chill thoroughly and serve with hot toast. (*Serves 4*)

Chicken Nanette

4 chicken breast portions (boned and sliced)
1 small onion (finely chopped)
1 medium green pepper (finely chopped)
¼ lb of button mushrooms (finely sliced)
2 egg yolks
½ pint of double cream
4 thin slices of Gruyère cheese
3 oz of butter
2 tablespoons of brandy
4 tablespoons of Madeira
A sprig of parsley
Salt, freshly milled black pepper

Melt the butter in a large and shallow flame-proof casserole, and gently sauté the onion, pepper and mushrooms for 10 minutes or so without letting them brown. Now add the seasoned chicken breasts and cook them on both sides to a pale gold (spoon off any excess butter or fat). Warm the brandy in a ladle, set light to it and pour it over the chicken, rotating the pan till the flames die down. Now add the Madeira, reduce the heat, cover and simmer very gently till the chicken is cooked – about 7 minutes.

Pre-heat the grill, then mix the egg yolks with the cream. Remove the pan from the heat and pour in the cream mixture, stirring it round to warm through in the hot pan. Now place a slice of Gruyère on top of each piece of chicken and melt it under the grill. Sprinkle with chopped parsley and serve immediately. (*Serves 4*)

Rhubarb Fool

1 lb of rhubarb
1 pint of double cream
1 oz of finely chopped preserved ginger
½ lb of caster sugar

In a heavy pan cook the rhubarb with the chopped ginger and caster sugar over a low heat with the lid on. There's no need to add any water. When the rhubarb is cooked, empty it into a large sieve, allow it to drain, then press it through into a clean bowl to make a purée. Leave to cool. Now whip the cream until it has just thickened, combine it with the rhubarb, then pour into individual glasses and chill thoroughly before serving. (*Serves 6 or 8*)

The Dundas Arms

Kintbury, Berkshire
Kintbury 263

Two hundred years ago this inn was known as the Red Lion, but during the Napoleonic wars it changed its name – less out of respect for Nelson's successor than out of tactful recognition of the fact that the crusty old admiral decided to take up residence down the road. But I doubt the inn ever actually needed the admiral's patronage. Long before he fought his last battle it was doing a roaring trade from the busy traffic of the Kennet and Avon canal which flows past its front door; even today it looks what it was originally intended to be – a congenial stopping place for the canal folk before they built Kintbury station next door (a rural halt where, amazingly, trains still occasionally stop in the heart of the Berkshire countryside).

Now the canal is open again and trout are fished in the Kennet, and over the past six years (under the Dalzell-Pipers) the Dundas Arms has justifiably recovered much of its former glory. The whole family cooks, it seems, though these recipes were produced by the son David, who also cooked us a meal one warm July day when the rose garden outside the dining room was ablaze with colour.

Cucumber Fritters with Dill and Soured Cream

4 oz of plain flour
A pinch of salt
3 tablespoons of olive oil
¼ pint of tepid water
1 level teaspoon of baking powder
1 large cucumber (peeled)
Oil (for deep frying)
Freshly milled black pepper, salt
Dried dill weed
¼ pint of soured cream

To make the sauce, boil a level teaspoon of dill in water for a few seconds, strain and add it to the soured cream with a seasoning of salt and pepper. Sift the flour and salt into a basin, make a well in the centre and add the oil; gradually add the tepid water, beating all the time until all the flour is incorporated and you have a smooth batter. The baking powder should be added just before you use the batter.

Cut the peeled cucumber into ¼-inch thick rounds, place in a colander, sprinkle with salt and leave them for an hour to drain. When you're ready to cook the fritters, rinse the cucumber in cold water and dry thoroughly in a clean cloth or kitchen paper. Dip the pieces in batter and deep-fry in hot oil (370°F) – if you don't have a cooking thermometer, test the oil by throwing in a cube of bread: if it froths and turns golden brown, it's ready. Cook the fritters till they're puffed and golden (you'll have to do them in several batches). Drain on kitchen paper, keep hot in the oven till all are done, sprinkle with salt and serve with the soured cream sauce. (*Serves 4 to 6*)

Scoblianka

A casserole of veal cooked with herbs and garnished with soured cream.

1½ lb of shoulder of veal
¾ lb of button mushrooms (sliced through to the stalks)
2 medium onions (sliced)
8 level tablespoons of butter
8 tablespoons of olive oil
Seasoned flour
1 level tablespoon of soft brown sugar
½ level teaspoon of dried dill weed
½ level teaspoon of dried sage
½ pint of chicken stock (see page 152)
3 tablespoons of soured cream
Salt, freshly milled black pepper

In a large heavy frying pan heat 2 tablespoons each of butter and oil, and lightly fry the mushrooms for about 5 minutes. Remove from the pan using a draining spoon and transfer into a large saucepan. Add some more butter and oil to the pan, then fry the onions till pale gold (they mustn't brown) and transfer them to the saucepan containing the mushrooms. Now cut the veal into ½-inch cubes, toss them in seasoned flour and again gently fry in butter and oil until lightly coloured but not too brown. You may need to do this in two lots depending on the size of your frying pan. Now transfer the veal to the saucepan. In another (small) saucepan, bring the sugar, dill, sage and 4 tablespoons of water to the boil, and pour this mixture over the veal. Add the chicken stock, bring to the boil, put on a lid and simmer gently for about an hour. Before serving stir in the soured cream and check the seasoning. (*Serves 4*)

Gooseberry Sorbet

2 lb of gooseberries
6 oz of caster sugar
1½ pints of water
The juice of a lemon
Green colouring
2 fl. oz of maraschino
2 fl. oz of white rum
3 elderflower heads (if available)

Cook the fruit with the sugar, water and the elderflowers. Add the lemon juice and green colouring, then pass the whole lot through the sieve. Turn the resultant purée into a container and put into the freezing compartment of the refrigerator. When it has thickened, add the maraschino and rum, stir and continue freezing till needed. This will not become too solid.

Thornbury Castle

Thornbury, Gloucestershire
Thornbury 2647

Kenneth Bell is the Crown Prince of restaurateurs, and Thornbury is his castle. He is, as we discovered on our travels, the one most looked up to by the others. Thornbury Castle, of course, has seen a long procession of famous owners since the days when Berthric snubbed Mathilda (later William the Conqueror's wife) and died in prison for it. Henry Stafford, the 2nd Duke of Buckingham, lived here till he foolishly attempted an insurrection against Richard III and had his head chopped off. The 3rd Duke of Buckingham, too, suffered a similar fate at the hands of Henry VIII, even before he had finished transforming it from a manor house into the present castle. Ann Boleyn spent ten days here in 1533 – and we know what happened to her.

But Kenneth Bell has proved that Thornbury Castle is not always so ill-omened. Since 1966 his restaurant here has flourished and re-established the formidable reputation he had previously earned at the Elizabeth in Oxford, and unlike former occupants he has incurred no royal disfavour (on the contrary, he was awarded the M.B.E. earlier this year for services to tourism – or as we prefer to think, to cooking in England). They have always eaten well at Thornbury ('For the Feast of the Nativity, 1507: 4 swans, 4 geese, 5 suckling pigs, 21 rabbits, 1 peacock . . .' etc.), and drunk well too. Records show the Staffords kept their own vineyard in the fifteenth century. That is another worthy tradition Kenneth Bell has revived; this Spring 2000 young vines in the grounds give promise of the first Thornbury vintage in 1975.

Avgolemono

A light lemon-flavoured soup from Greece.

2 pints of well-seasoned chicken stock (see page 152)
2 oz of long-grain rice
4 large fresh eggs
4 dessertspoons of lemon juice
Salt, freshly milled black pepper

Bring the chicken stock to the boil, throw in the rice and simmer until the rice grains are tender. Now taste and season with salt and freshly milled black pepper (it should be rather more salty than you'd expect, as it will be diluted with the eggs and lemon juice). In a large bowl beat the eggs together quite thoroughly with the lemon juice, then pour the boiling stock over the eggs, whisking vigorously at the same time (a balloon whisk or electric hand whisk would be best for this). Now return the mixture to the hot saucepan and reheat carefully, without allowing the eggs to scramble. Serve immediately, while still frothy, in warmed soup bowls. (*Serves 4*)

Salmon Coulibiac

For the pastry (to be made the day before):
2 eggs
10 oz of plain flour
½ oz of yeast
2 oz of butter
½ level teaspoon of sugar
4 tablespoons of milk
A pinch of salt

Place the sugar and yeast in a bowl and cream them together to a liquid, beat up the eggs, add them to the yeast then gently heat the milk to lukewarm and pour it into the egg and yeast mixture (it's most important not to overheat the milk: more than 100°F will kill the yeast). Sift the flour and salt into a large mixing bowl, then rub in the butter with your fingertips. Pour in the yeast mixture and knead thoroughly; then cover the bowl with a clean cloth and allow the dough to rise in a warm place for 45 minutes. When risen, store the dough in a polythene bag in the refrigerator until the next day. (*Serves 4*)

For the filling:
8 oz of fresh salmon
3 oz of long-grain rice
2 oz of small white mushrooms (thinly sliced)
1½ oz of onions (finely chopped)
Butter for frying
2 eggs
8 fl. oz of strongly seasoned fish stock (see page 152)
2 oz of butter
2 tablespoons of breadcrumbs
1 rounded tablespoon of fresh chopped parsley
1 dessertspoon of fresh chopped tarragon
Salt, freshly milled black pepper
A little milk

Pre-heat the oven to 300°F (mark 2).

Wrap the salmon in a well buttered piece of foil and seal well. Place it on a baking sheet and half-cook it in the oven for about 10 to 15 minutes. Place the eggs in cold water, bring them to the boil, boil for 7 minutes exactly then cool under a cold running tap. Now bring the stock to simmering point, throw in the rice, stir once, and cook gently till the rice is tender and all the stock has been absorbed. Fry the onion and mushroom in butter, mix them into the rice, then set all the ingredients aside to cool. Now roll out the pastry into 2 rectangles approximately ⅛ inch thick, making one slightly larger than the other. Paint the edges of the smaller rectangle with milk, then spread the rice mixture evenly over it (leaving the edges clear), cover the rice with the flaked salmon, then the sliced hard-boiled eggs, parsley and tarragon, finally top this with 2 oz of butter cut into slices.

Now lay the other pastry rectangle over this and seal the edges well all round. Place the Coulibiac on a buttered baking sheet, make some small slits in the top, then paint the top with melted butter and sprinkle with breadcrumbs. Bake in a pre-heated oven 400°F (mark 6) for about 25 minutes or until the pastry is a good colour and the Coulibiac is heated through inside. Serve with a jug of melted butter. (*Serves 4*)

Raspberry Shortcake

1 lb of prepared raspberries
8 oz of plain flour
5 oz of soft brown sugar
3 oz of butter (room temperature)
1 level teaspoon of baking powder
1 level dessertspoon of caster sugar

Pre-heat the oven to 350°F (mark 4).

Arrange the prepared raspberries in a fireproof dish and sprinkle with caster sugar. Then sift the flour and baking powder into a bowl, rub in the butter lightly until the mixture is all crumbly, then mix the brown sugar in. Cover the raspberries with the crumbled pastry, sprinkling it on lightly without pressing down, smooth the surface evenly, and bake for 25 to 30 minutes. This is excellent served either hot or cold with fresh cream. (*Serves 4*)

Stuffed Aubergines

4 aubergines (about 1½ lb)
Salt
Oil
2 level tablespoons of butter
4 medium onions (chopped)
1 level tablespoon of paprika
3 large tomatoes (peeled and chopped)
2 level tablespoons of tomato purée
1 teaspoon of Worcester sauce
½ level teaspoon of dried oregano
3 oz of white crab meat
3 oz of brown crab meat
1 egg (beaten)
4 level tablespoons of freshly grated Parmesan
Salt and freshly milled black pepper

Slice the aubergines in half lengthways, make shallow criss-cross cuts in the white flesh of each half, sprinkle with salt and leave on one side for about 30 minutes. Pre-heat the oven to 350°F (mark 4). Squeeze the excess moisture out of the aubergines, dry them a bit with kitchen paper, then arrange them (cut side up) on a foil-lined baking tin, brush the cut surfaces with oil, and bake for 30 to 45 minutes or until they are quite soft. Then remove them from the oven and turn the heat up to 400°F (mark 6).

When the aubergines are cool enough to handle, scoop out the flesh with a teaspoon, leaving the skins intact. Put the skins back in a roasting tin and chop the flesh finely. In a saucepan, sauté the onion in butter till soft, then stir in the paprika, chopped aubergine flesh, tomatoes, tomato purée and Worcester sauce and oregano. Stir well and cook (uncovered) fairly slowly until the

Cleeveway House

Bishop's Cleeve, Gloucestershire
Bishop's Cleeve 2585

Years ago Sir Frank Whittle chose this house to get away from his jet engines, and if you're lucky enough (like us) to be driving up for dinner as the sunset is blushing the mellow seventeenth-century limestone, you'll see why. But long before that Bishop's Cleeve was a sort of country retreat, I suppose you'd call it, for former bishops of Gloucester, and Cleeveway House was where they, too, came for their relaxation. Gourmandising prelates would still be welcome of course, but in these more democratic days this Cotswold outpost is a refuge for *all* good food lovers.

For the past seven years here John Marfell (another protégé of The Hole-in-the-Wall) and his wife have been infecting the area with their enthusiasm for food, and rejoicing it with meticulous cooking (Mr Marfell even hangs all his own meat). The doorless kitchen almost invites you to spy on his art. And if you've never seen a groaning board face to face, observe the Cold Table as you enter the dining room, and see if you can walk past unmoved. It is truly episcopal.

mixture is reduced to a thick consistency. Taste to check the seasoning, then combine the mixture with the crab meats and one beaten egg. Stuff the aubergine skins, sprinkle with Parmesan cheese and return them to the hot oven to brown – this takes about 10 minutes – then serve at once. (*Serves 8*)

Barbecued Pork Fillet with Fried Rice

4 pork tenderloins
Salt and freshly milled black pepper
Butter for frying

For the sauce:
2 oz of butter
1 medium onion (chopped small)
¼ pint of stock
3 large tomatoes (peeled and chopped)
1 tablespoon of Worcester sauce
2 tablespoons of soy sauce
4 level tablespoons of home-made tomato sauce (see page 151)
1 tablespoon of honey
1 teaspoon of French mustard
Freshly milled black pepper

For the fried rice:
6 oz of long-grain rice (boiled for 5 minutes and refreshed under cold water)
1 green pepper (finely chopped)
1 medium onion (finely chopped)
Oil for frying
4 oz of peeled prawns
4 oz of bacon
2 tablespoons of fresh chopped parsley
Soy sauce
Freshly milled black pepper, salt
Parsley

First make the sauce by melting the butter and gently frying the onion in it for about 10 minutes. Then add the stock and the chopped tomatoes. Simmer for a minute or two, then add the tomato, soy and Worcester sauces and the honey, and season well with freshly milled black pepper and only a little salt (as there's some in the soy sauce). This mixture should be left to simmer slowly without a lid until it has reduced by half, then add the mustard and taste to check the seasoning. Pre-heat the oven to 375°F (mark 5).

The pork tenderloin should be cut into ¼-inch slices, seasoned with salt and freshly milled pepper, then fried gently in a little butter till just brown (you'll need your largest frying pan for this). Pour the reduced sauce over the pork fillets, bring to simmering point, then pour into a casserole. Cover with buttered paper and cook in the oven for 12 minutes. Meanwhile prepare the fried rice.

Fry the chopped onion in a little olive oil in a frying pan over a high heat, add the chopped pepper and bacon and cook for a few minutes, shaking the pan to prevent every-

thing sticking. Add the cooked rice and prawns and about 1½ to 2 tablespoons of soy sauce. Cook for about 4 minutes, remove from the heat and taste to check the seasoning. Serve the rice on a plate sprinkled with chopped parsley, with the pork and sauce arranged on top. (*Serves 8*)

Chestnut Turinois

8 oz of unsalted butter (room temperature)
4 oz of icing sugar
8 oz of plain chocolate
1 heaped tablespoon of instant coffee dissolved in 1 tablespoon of hot water
2 tablespoons of rum
14 oz of sweetened chestnut purée
½ pint of double cream (whipped)
2 oz of flaked toasted almonds

Use a sandwich tin 8 inches round by 1½ inches deep; line the base with foil and lightly grease the base and sides of the tin with a tasteless oil (groundnut). Break up the chocolate and melt it in a basin over hot water (or in a warm oven). Cream the butter and icing sugar together until smooth, light and fluffy (this is best done with an electric mixer), then beat in the chestnut purée, coffee and rum and finally the melted chocolate. Beat thoroughly to blend everything together. Pour the mixture into the prepared tin, smooth it evenly with the back of a spoon, then cover with foil and chill through till firm. To serve, slide a knife all round the edge to loosen, turn out on to a serving plate, cover with whipped cream, decorate with toasted almonds, and serve cut in wedges. (*Serves 8*)

The Close

Tetbury, Gloucestershire
Tetbury 272

There is almost nothing you can do on a horse which isn't done within a gallop of Tetbury; jumping at Badminton, polo at Cirencester, racing at Cheltenham, even hunting at the Duke of Beaufort's. But the town itself has one overwhelming attraction: the Close, a splendid sixteenth-century building just down the road from the mediaeval town hall. From the street it has the dignity of a typical Elizabethan wool merchant's home (which it once was), but from the garden its cloistral calm is more reminiscent of the Cistercian monastery from which it probably originated. Inside, however, the rooms are handsomely Georgian, perfectly proportioned, with Adam ceilings and carved fireplaces. The result is one of comfortable elegance – an elusive combination, but something that strikes you immediately about John and Peggy Hastings' hotel.

They like to think of it more as a friendly home than as a hotel. And so it is. You are welcome to wander into the kitchen to compliment the cook Alan Thong (which you'll certainly want to do) and you'll be greeted with smiles no matter how busy they are. If Mrs Hastings' kitchen is full of youthful inventiveness, then Mr Hastings' wines – as you'd expect from a Chevalier du Tastevin – are the essence of mature judgement.

Celery and Almond Soup

1 head of celery
1 medium onion
4 oz of sweet almonds (blanched and skinned)
2 pints of chicken stock (see page 152)
½ pint of milk
1½ oz of butter
1½ oz of flour
6 teaspoons of double cream
3 level teaspoons of ground almonds
Salt, freshly milled pepper

Chop the sticks of celery fairly small, and do the same with the almonds and onion, then simmer all these together in the seasoned stock for about an hour – and then press the whole lot through a Mouli or a sieve. Now melt the butter in a saucepan, stir in the flour till smooth, then stir in the purée bit by bit until everything is smooth and thoroughly blended. Now add the milk and bring to simmering point – still stirring. Taste to check the seasoning. Serve with a teaspoon of cream and a sprinkling of ground almonds on each bowl of soup. (*Serves* 6)

Le Gigot d'Agneau Bédouin

1 leg of English lamb (boned)
3 oz of butter
½ a loaf of fresh white bread
2 tablespoons of runny honey
½ a lemon (juice and zest)
1 oz of flaked almonds
1 oz of sultanas
4 oz of stoned and chopped dates
1 large egg (beaten)
5 fl. oz (approx) of milk
½ level teaspoon of oregano
1 level teaspoon of cumin
2 level teaspoons of coriander
½ level teaspoon of ground black pepper
1½ level teaspoons of sea salt
Seasoned flour

Pre-heat the oven to 400°F (mark 6).

First cut the crusts off the bread and make the loaf into breadcrumbs – either by hand or preferably in a liquidiser. Combine the breadcrumbs with the almonds, sultanas, dates and all the herbs and seasonings. Add the grated rind and the juice of the lemon, then add melted butter, milk and egg, and stir thoroughly until well blended – the mixture should be fairly moist, so add a little more milk if you think it needs it. Now pack this stuffing into the lamb in the place where the bone was taken out, and sew up into a neat joint with a larding needle and pack thread. Dust the joint with seasoned flour and smear the

honey (warmed first) all over. Now place the joint in a roasting pan containing a ½ inch of water, and bake on the bottom of the oven for 20 minutes, then reduce the temperature to 375°F (mark 5) and cook until tender (approximately 2 to 2½ hours altogether. (*Servings according to size of joint*)

Clafoutis Limousin

1½ lb of black cherries (pitted)
3 level tablespoons of caster sugar
A pinch of salt
8 oz of plain flour
3 large eggs (separated)
8 fl. oz of milk *and*
2 fl. oz of water mixed together
3 drops of vanilla essence
½ oz of butter
Kirsch or brandy

Pre-heat the oven to gas mark 4 (350°F).

Butter a large, wide and shallow ovenproof dish. Sift the flour and salt into a bowl, make a well in the centre and drop in the 3 egg yolks. Add some of the milk-and-water until it's all in and you have a smooth batter. Beat very well (as for Yorkshire Pudding), adding the vanilla essence, then leave the batter to stand in the fridge for about an hour. At the same time place the cherries in the baking dish and sprinkle them with half the caster sugar and 1 tablespoon of Kirsch or brandy. When you're ready to cook the Clafoutis, beat the egg whites until stiff, then carefully fold them into the batter, using a metal spoon. Now pour the batter over the cherries, sprinkle on the rest of the sugar and bake in the oven until well risen and golden brown. Sprinkle on a little more liqueur before serving. This can be eaten hot or cold, but is best served slightly warm, with pouring cream. (*Serves 6*)

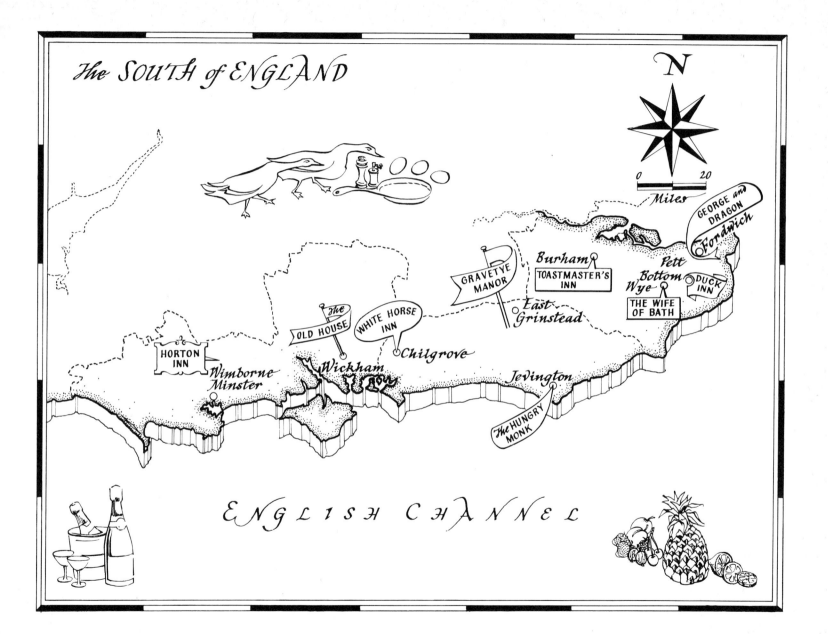

Duck Inn

Pett Bottom, Kent
Bridge 354

In the days before the last war when the Pett Valley still rang to the wood-cutter's axe and wood auctions were a weekly feature of the local halls, this inn was called, naturally enough, the Wood-man's Arms. Originally two farm cottages built in 1640, it was licensed in the 1880s to supply the forestry trade with beer and shoelaces. Now the trees and the woodmen have gone and the old inn sign reads Duck – not from a profusion of small birds but from the cry that rang out as patrons stumbled round the well at the entrance and through the four-foot-six-inch door: Duck!

You might wonder what brings people

nowadays up this lonely road to nowhere (except other Bottoms) if you didn't know about Mrs Laing's cooking, which has been known in fact to bring them over from France for Sunday lunch. Ulla may be Swedish, but if the last meal a returning Frenchman eats before embarking at Dover is one of her distinctive dinners, she's a great advertisement for cooking in England.

Brandade

12 oz of poached cod fillet (weighed when all skin and bones removed)
4 oz of white breadcrumbs (taken from the inside of a day-old loaf)
¼ pint of mayonnaise
8 cloves of garlic
1 level tablespoon of salt
Freshly milled black pepper
The juice of ½ lemon
Sprigs of watercress (for garnish)

Peel the garlic, crush each clove and mix it to a paste with a level tablespoon of salt and freshly milled black pepper (8 full turns). Add the cod and mash with a fork to a fine paste. Add the crumbs, mayonnaise and lemon juice and continue mixing till you have a smooth paste without any lumps. Pack the mixture into a terrine or serving dish, cover with foil and chill. Mrs Laing suggests that this dish should be made at least 2 days ahead, as it improves with keeping. Serve with sprigs of watercress as garnish and croûtons, crusty bread or hot toast. (*Serves 6*)

Chicken Ulla

1 fresh chicken (3 ¼ to 3 ½ lb)
The juice of 1 lemon
1 pint of chicken stock (see page 152)
1 onion (cut into quarters)
1 leek (cleaned and cut into slices)
2 carrots (pared and sliced)
Bouquet garni (made with a bay leaf, a sprig of thyme, sprig of parsley, tied together with string)
2 oz of butter
2 oz of plain flour
¼ pint of dry French Vermouth
¼ pint of double cream
¾ lb of button mushrooms (wiped, thinly sliced)
A little extra butter and Vermouth
Freshly milled black pepper, ground rock salt

Rub the chicken inside and out with fresh lemon juice (this helps to keep it white). Place it in a suitably sized saucepan together with the vegetables and bouquet garni, and season with freshly milled black pepper and rock salt. Pour in the stock, put a lid on and simmer gently for ¾ to 1 hour or until tender. Towards the end of the cooking time, start to prepare the sauce in a second pan by melting the butter and stirring in the flour to make a thick white roux. When the chicken is cooked remove it to a warmed serving dish, carve and keep it warm. Strain off ¼ of a pint of the cooking liquid and add it a little at a time to the roux, followed by ¼ of a pint of Vermouth (also added very gradually). Turn the heat to very low and allow the sauce to cook for a few minutes. Then toss the sliced mushrooms into some melted butter and a tablespoon of Vermouth in a frying pan, and cook them lightly (they should be fairly 'al dente'). Now pour the mushrooms and their juice into the sauce, stir and finally add the cream. Taste to check the seasoning. When the cream is heated through, pour the sauce over the chicken. (*Serves 4*)

Pears in Cassis

6 fairly hard dessert pears (peeled)
½ bottle of rough red wine
6 oz of granulated sugar
3 cloves
1 small strip of lemon rind
1 small cinnamon stick
2 fl. oz of Cassis (blackcurrant liqueur)
2 tablespoons of brandy

For the Crème Chantilly.
½ pint of double cream
1 level dessertspoon of caster sugar
1 or 2 tablespoons of Cassis

Pre-heat the oven to 325°F (mark 3).

Boil the wine, sugar and flavouring ingredients together until the mixture is reduced by about a half and has taken on the consistency of syrup. Arrange the pears in a baking dish, pour the syrup over, put on a tight lid and bake for approximately 1½ hours, or until the pears are tender (turn them over a couple of times during the cooking). Cool and chill thoroughly before serving, and serve with the cream, sugar and Cassis whipped to a light Crème Chantilly. (*Serves 6*)

George and Dragon

Fordwich, Kent
Canterbury 710661

It was once the right of the keeper of this low-beamed inn to collect tolls from travellers across the little stone bridge over the Stour. But a great deal has changed since the estuary was wide enough to accommodate a busy river traffic (including Julius Caesar's invasion fleet) and this privilege has disappeared, along with the village's right to elect its own member of Parliament. Still, the George and Dragon fortunately has not been hustled into precipitate change: the dining room is still as pew-like as an eighteenth-century chop-house, and even the Paris fashions on the coffee-room wall were all the rage in the nineteenth century. More important still, in the kitchen Mr and Mrs Pardoe and their chefs Victoria Keem, Jacqueline Dadds and Alison Page uphold the traditional virtues of flavoursome, well-hung meat, proper respect for all vegetables, and patience with the stockpot.

Deep-fried Mushrooms with Cucumber Sauce

8 large open dark-gilled mushrooms
½ cucumber (peeled and chopped small)
½ onion (finely chopped)
1 tablespoon of finely chopped watercress
½ pint of home-made mayonnaise (see page 151)
1 level tablespoon of seasoned flour
1 egg (beaten)
3 tablespoons of dried breadcrumbs
4 crisp lettuce leaves
½ lemon (cut into wedges)
Oil
Salt, freshly milled black pepper

Mix the cucumber, watercress and chopped onion thoroughly with the mayonnaise and pour the mixture into a serving dish. The mushrooms should be dipped first in flour, then in egg, and finally in breadcrumbs pressed well in to obtain a good even coating. Deep-fry the mushrooms in hot oil till golden brown, drain well on kitchen paper, season with salt and pepper, and serve

on crisp lettuce leaves, garnished with lemon. Serve the sauce separately. (*Serves 4*)

Suprême de Volaille Farcie

Ask the butcher to bone out 2 chickens and provide you with 4 skinned breast portions beaten out until thin but not broken.

For the stuffing:
2 oz of butter
¼ lb of mushrooms (chopped)
1 onion (chopped)
¼ pint of dry white wine
2 level teaspoons of dried tarragon
The juice of ½ lemon
½ lb of fresh white breadcrumbs
¼ lb of chopped ham
Salt, freshly milled black pepper
Flour, beaten egg and breadcrumbs to coat
Oil for frying
Lemon and lettuce to garnish

In a frying pan melt the butter and fry the onion till soft, then add the mushrooms, cook for a further 5 minutes then add the tarragon, lemon juice, wine and a seasoning of salt and freshly milled pepper. Cook for a further 5 minutes, then stir in the breadcrumbs to absorb all the juices, and finally stir in the ham. Spoon the stuffing a little on each chicken breast, roll them up and press together to seal. Dip each portion in flour, then in beaten egg, and lastly in breadcrumbs and deep-fry in medium hot oil for about 10 minutes till crisp and golden brown. Serve garnished with lemon quarters and crisp lettuce leaves. (*Serves 4*)

Butterscotch Pie

A 9- or 10-inch pastry case baked blind
3 egg yolks
A pinch of salt
6 oz of demerara sugar
3 heaped tablespoons of cornflour
3 teaspoons of vanilla essence
¼ lb of salted butter
1 pint of milk

For the meringue:
3 egg whites
6 oz of caster sugar

Combine the egg yolks and sugar by beating them until pale in colour, then mix the salt and cornflour with a little cold water till smooth, and add it to the egg yolk mixture. Now pour the whole mixture into a double saucepan, stir in the milk and whisk over simmering water (a balloon whisk is best for this) until the mixture is really thick and the whisk stands up by itself. Remove the top part of the saucepan from the heat, add the butter and vanilla essence, and stir occasionally until the mixture has cooled. Then pour the butterscotch into the prepared pastry case and leave it to set a little. For the topping, whisk the egg whites till they form soft peaks, then gradually whisk in the sugar, about 1 oz at a time. Pile the meringue on top of the butterscotch, taking it right up to the pastry rim to seal, then bake it in a low oven (250°F (mark ½) until the meringue is golden and crisp – about 30 minutes or so. (*Serves 4 to 6*)

Toastmaster's Inn

Burham, Kent
Medway 61299

Just a glance at the senior Mr Ward
behind the bar of the Toastmaster's and
you needn't ask how this inn got its
name. Suffice it to say he is president-
elect of the Society of London Toast-
masters, a freeman of the City of London,
cheery and joking ('I do cremations as
well') – the epitome of hospitality. He
says his son Gregory is too modest, and
so he is. The food at the Toastmaster's is
his province and, far from just being
there to supplement the wine, it is
original and adventurous.

All the same, their cellars are a wonder to
behold. When we arrived the first volume
of the wine list (France and Germany) had
just been revised. It was a thick tome and
there wasn't time to read all through each
vintage, but we noticed that the clarets
went back to 1860 (a bottle of unknown
origin from Rudding Park) with few of the
breaks that you might expect. It must be
one of the best privately owned cellars
in the country.

58

Nettle Soup

Mr Ward junior recommends that gloves are worn when gathering the nettles. The soup, he says, has 'a taste of the hedgerows'.

2 lb of nettles (only the top growth)
2 pints of good chicken stock
4 oz of butter
2 lb of potatoes (peeled and chopped small)
A little milk
4 tablespoons of double cream
1 tablespoon of chopped chervil
Salt, freshly milled black pepper

Blanch the nettles by pouring boiling water over them, then strain carefully and press all the water out. Melt the butter in a thick saucepan, stir in the nettles, put a lid on and let them sweat gently for 10 minutes or so. Then stir in the potatoes, add the stock, replace the lid and simmer gently for 25 minutes or until the potatoes are soft. Either liquidise or sieve the mixture, and if you think it needs it add a little boiling milk to bring it to the right consistency (not too thin). Taste to check the seasoning, then finally re-heat, stir in the cream and chervil and serve. (*Serves* 6)

Tranche d'Agneau à la Catalane

Lamb steaks marinaded for two days – if you can wait that long.

6 lamb steaks (about an inch thick, cut from the top of the leg)

For the marinade:
½ pint of good olive oil (preferably Provençale)
6 large cloves of garlic (crushed)
1 good handful of fresh thyme leaves (or 1 tablespoon if dried)
1 large onion (finely sliced)
24 peppercorns

Place the lamb steaks side by side in a large oblong dish or tin. Crush the garlic and rub it over the meat, then slightly crush the peppercorns (either in a pestle and mortar or with the back of a tablespoon) and sprinkle over the meat with thyme and onion. Then pour in the oil and leave it all in a cool place to marinade for at least a day – though preferably two – turning them over now and then. To cook them, wipe most of the oil away, get a thick frying pan (probably two frying pans) very hot, and sear the steaks on both sides to a good brown, then cook according to how you like them. (*Serves* 6)

The Wife of Bath

Wye, Kent
Wye 540

Hidden among the hop fields and orchards, the village of Wye has an unmistakably artistic feeling to it. Pottery, you feel sure, is made here, and paintings for every taste. Michael Waterfield has been known to wield the pen and brush, but to the world at large his artistry with food is better known. Nine years ago he took over this ancient house and created the Wife of Bath out of it – not only in celebration of Chaucer's bawdy pilgrims, but also of George Perry-Smith's former restaurant the Hole in the Wall in Bath, where, like many others in this book, he once trained.

Food, you might say, runs in the family; at the time of Mrs Beeton, his great-great-aunt wrote a best-seller on vegetable cooking which her great-great-nephew has just updated and illustrated. But Michael's way with French provincial cooking is all his own and rightly famous. Local produce has always been used at the Wife of Bath; but with a benevolent sun, it may not be long before it can boast its own local wine – when Mr Waterfield's vineyard goes into production next year.

Sole au Vert-Pré

6 fillets of sole (weighing about 4 oz each)
6 spring onions (cleaned and chopped)
1 handful each of fresh spinach and sorrel leaves (finely chopped)
1 heaped tablespoon each of fresh chopped parsley, marjoram and chervil
6 green peppercorns
2 oz of butter
¾ oz of flour
3 fl. oz of dry white wine
¼ pint of water
¼ pint of double cream
Some extra butter
Salt, freshly milled black pepper

Pre-heat the oven to 375°F (mark 5).

Just before serving, butter a baking tin and arrange the sole fillets side by side in it. Add a few flecks of butter, cover with a buttered piece of foil and bake for 10 minutes.

To make the sauce, sweat the chopped spring onions in the butter, stir in the flour, then add all the chopped herbs and gradually stir in the wine and water till smooth and thickened. Now add peppercorns, spinach and sorrel, plus a little salt, and simmer gently for 10 minutes. Then whizz to a purée in an electric blender (or pass through a sieve), return to the saucepan, add the cream and stir over a gentle heat till heated through, keep warm. Arrange the sole on a warmed serving dish, and serve with the sauce poured over. (*Serves 6*)

Chicken Jurasienne

2 fresh chickens (3 to 3½ lb each)
  Ask the butcher to bone the chicken and divide each one into 4 portions, remove the skin and flatten. Ask for the bones, skins and giblet as well.

For the stuffing:
2 chicken livers
½ onion (chopped)
4 oz of lean minced pork
1 dessertspoon of fresh chopped tarragon (or 1 teaspoon if dried)
1 tablespoon of brandy
1 tablespoon of cream
Salt, freshly milled black pepper

For the chicken:
2 oz of butter
3 medium onions (chopped)
4 carrots (sliced)
½ bottle of Jura (or any other dry white) wine
¾ pint of chicken stock (made with the bones, skin, etc.)
1 chicken stock cube
1 sprig of tarragon
1 oz of butter and 1 oz of flour, blended to make beurre manié
¼ pint of double cream
Salt, freshly milled black pepper

Mince the chicken livers and combine them with the rest of the stuffing ingredients. Place a good tablespoon of stuffing on each piece of chicken, then roll the chicken round the stuffing (keeping the ends in when rolling) and tie the pieces up with string. Now take a large, heavy flameproof casserole and in it fry the pieces of chicken in the butter until they are golden on all sides. Remove the chicken and set aside, then fry the onion and carrots to soften for about 10 minutes. Now replace the chicken, pour ½ a bottle of wine in, add the chicken stock plus a crumbled chicken stock cube and a sprig of tarragon, and season with freshly ground black pepper. Put the lid on and poach gently for 30 minutes or until the chicken is tender. Remove the chicken pieces and vegetables to a warmed serving dish, take off the string and keep warm. Boil the liquid fast to reduce it by half, then thicken with the beurre manié added in peanut-sized pieces. Bring to the boil again, add the cream, adjust the seasoning, pour the sauce over the chicken, and serve. (Serves 8)

Coffee and Almond Tart

An 8-inch flan case made with shortcrust pastry, partly cooked
4 egg yolks
1½ oz of sugar
1½ oz of freshly roasted coffee beans
¾ pint of cream

For the topping:
2 egg whites (large)
1½ oz of flaked almonds, toasted
1½ oz of caster sugar

First of all, the coffee beans should be ground coarsely in a pestle and mortar (or failing that a mincer). Place the ground coffee in a saucepan, add the cream and heat it very slowly without letting it come to the boil. Then remove from the heat and allow to infuse till cold. Beat the egg yolks and sugar, pour the coffee cream through a fine nylon sieve and beat it into the yolks. Place the flan case on a baking sheet and pour in the mixture and bake at 375°F (mark 5) until just set – 25 to 30 minutes.

Turn the heat up to 425°F (mark 7). Beat the egg whites until stiff, beat in the sugar bit by bit, then fold in the almonds. Pile the mixture on top of the custard, sealing well round the edges by taking the meringue mixture right up to the pastry rim, and bake in the oven for a few minutes to brown nicely. Serve slightly warm or cold. (Serves 4 to 6)

Gravetye Manor

Turner's Hill, East Grinstead, Sussex
Sharpthorne 567

Gravetye Manor was built in 1598 by Roger Infield for his bride Katherine, and their initials are scattered still about their love-nest. Smugglers have since used the house for less romantic purposes (part of Smugglers Lane remains in the estate) but it is – as it always has been – a haven of good taste. The grounds are the work of William Robinson, a former occupant and the foremost landscape gardener of the Victorian age, who persisted in scattering seeds and bulbs even from his wheelchair. Their charm and variety are assiduously preserved today and they have provided the model for many other natural gardens in England and indeed throughout the world.

Such houses are inevitably a reflection of their incumbent, and it is a happy chance that the present one should be Peter Herbert, whose knowledge of food and wine (and, we discovered, of food and wine writers) has added yet another facet to the manor's character. Every now and then the fortunate few who belong to the country club are treated to bargain wine auctions and 'regional feasts'. And those who simply come here as hotel guests will also discover that the Austrian chef's impressive skills are not confined to Vienna.

Champignons Farcis Frits 'Gravetye'

16 medium dark-gilled field mushroom caps
2 medium shallots (chopped small)
½ medium green pepper (de-seeded, chopped small)
2 oz of smoked ham (chopped small)
1 oz of Gruyère cheese (diced)
1 oz of Cheddar cheese (grated)
2 heaped tablespoons of soft white breadcrumbs
1 dessertspoon of brandy
3 fl. oz of red wine
1 tablespoon of fresh snipped chives
Salt, freshly milled black pepper
Seasoned flour
Oil for deep frying
1 beaten egg
Dried breadcrumbs
Parsley
Lemon quarters
Tartare sauce

First place the chopped shallots in a saucepan with the chopped pepper, ham and wine, and simmer till the vegetables are tender (about 20 minutes). Then stir into the hot mixture the chives, Gruyère, Cheddar, fresh breadcrumbs and brandy, season and place a tablespoonful of this mixture onto each mushroom half. Now take pairs of similar size

and press firmly together. Dip each first in flour, then in the beaten egg and lastly in breadcrumbs, making sure they all get a good coating. Deep-fry in medium hot (370°F) cooking oil till golden, drain on crumpled kitchen paper and serve garnished with parsley, lemon quarters and Tartare sauce. (*Serves 4*)

Austrian Braised Red Cabbage

A truly authentic recipe from Carl Loderer, Gravetye's Austrian chef.

1 medium red cabbage (shredded finely)
1 large onion (chopped small)
1 tablespoon of redcurrant jelly
3½ fl. oz of red wine
4 rashers of streaky bacon (chopped small)
1 small cooking apple (peeled and grated)
4 tablespoons of red wine vinegar
4 level tablespoons of brown sugar
4 cloves
A bay leaf
Salt, freshly milled black pepper

Pre-heat the oven to 325°F (mark 3).

Place the cabbage, onion and apple in an ovenproof casserole; add the redcurrant jelly, red wine, bay leaf and bacon. In a small saucepan boil the vinegar with the sugar and cloves until the vinegar is reduced by half. Pour it, through a strainer, over the casserole ingredients, and add about 4 tablespoons of water; season. Put a lid on the casserole and cook in the oven for 2 hours stirring occasionally. Red cabbage cooked in this way can be re-heated the next day without any ill effects. (*Serves 4*)

Saltzburger Nockerln

A deliciously light 'mountain' shaped soufflé, flavoured with orange and lemon and flamed in rum.

8 egg whites
4 oz of granulated sugar
The finely grated zest of 1 lemon and 1 orange
1 heaped tablespoon of plain flour
4 egg yolks
½ level teaspoon of vanilla sugar
1 dessertspoon of thick honey
2 fl. oz of rum
1 fl. oz of double cream

Pre-heat the oven to 400°F (mark 6).

Place the honey and the cream in an 8-inch soufflé dish and put on the lowest shelf in the oven. Meanwhile whisk the egg whites till stiff, then slowly beat in the granulated sugar and continue beating until the sugar has dissolved. Beat the egg yolks lightly and fold them carefully into the meringue mixture, adding the orange and lemon zest and the vanilla sugar (or sugar plus a drop or two of vanilla essence). Finally add the sifted flour, folding in very gently. Next remove the hot soufflé dish from the oven and spoon the meringue over the melted honey and cream, piling the mixture up into a mountain shape. Place the dish back in the oven and cook for 20 minutes or until the mixture is golden brown and firm to touch. Put the hot dish on a serving place, heat a ladle of rum, set light to it and pour the flaming rum over the 'mountain' at the table. Serve at once. (*Serves 4*)

The Hungry Monk

Jevington, Sussex
Polegate 2178

If there *are* any hungry monks in Jevington, then they are the ghosts of former inmates of the monastery which, it is supposed, once stood in the field by Church Lane. For no man – religious or profane – leaves Nigel and Susan Mackenzie's ancient beamed, Sussex-flinted restaurant hungry. Five years ago the Mackenzies decided they wanted to work in the country, agreed they liked entertaining, and very logically opened a country restaurant. Success has been swift, and well merited. Their hospitality extends even to a free glass of port after your dinner, and their kitchen is genuinely creative.

But above all, they so obviously find the whole thing such fun – as is witnessed by the little cook book they have found time to write and have published privately. It reveals the *Secrets of the Hungry Monk* (who, drawn by the cartoonist Graham, prowls about its pages in jolly aprons and devours learned texts on the feeding of the five thousand). The menu below is extracted (gratefully) from the book, but if you want to find out the other recipes, you couldn't do better than make the pilgrimage to Jevington yourself and buy a copy.

Kippers in Cream and Curry Sauce

1 lb of kipper fillets
1 bay leaf
2 oz of butter
1 level dessertspoon of curry powder
1 small eating apple
2 oz of flour
8 fl. oz of double cream

Poach the kipper fillets in 1½ pints of water with a bay leaf. Melt the butter in a saucepan, and grate the apple straight into the butter, then add the curry powder. Sprinkle in the flour (to make a roux) and stir for 2 or 3 minutes. Gradually pour in 1 pint of the stock from the poached kippers and bring to the boil, stirring briskly. Simmer for 15 minutes, remove from the heat and blend in 5 fl. oz cream. Flake in the kippers, and ladle the mixture into 4 individual dishes or ramekins. Pour a spoonful of cream onto the top of each dish and flash under the grill. Serve immediately. (*Serves 4*)

Rare Beef Pancakes

3 lb of sirloin of beef (boned and trimmed)
8 pancakes (see page 153 for batter)
1 lb of liver pâté
Some dripping
1 clove of garlic
Salt, freshly milled black pepper

For the sauce:
1 oz of butter
6 oz of mushrooms
6 oz of tomatoes
1 onion
1 fl. oz of brandy
1 glass of white wine
1 pint of espagnole sauce (see page 152)
1 clove of garlic

Pre-heat the oven to 425°F (mark 7).

First make the pancakes and keep them warm, and take the pâté out of the refrigerator. Wipe and chop the mushrooms; skin and chop the tomatoes and peel and chop the onion. Roast the beef (seasoned with salt and freshly milled black pepper) with 1 clove of crushed garlic and dotted with dripping, in an open roasting tray. Depending on how rare you like your beef, cook for anything between 35 minutes and 1 hour.
Meanwhile melt the butter in a pan and cook the onion and garlic till brown. Toss in the tomatoes and mushrooms and continue frying till soft, then add the brandy and flambé. Pour in the white wine, turn up the heat and let it bubble until reduced by half. Now add the espagnole sauce, stirring constantly. Cover the pan and simmer gently. Just before serving, carve the steak into 16 slices and lay two on each pancake together with 2 oz of pâté. Roll up and quickly pour the wine sauce over, and serve at once. (*Serves 8*)

Chocolate and Orange Cheesecake

4 oz of wheatmeal biscuits
1 oz of butter
¼ lb of plain Bournville chocolate
1½ lb of cream cheese
3 fl. oz of concentrated Birds Eye Florida orange juice (thawed)
2 oz of caster sugar

Crumble the biscuits, and melt the chocolate with a little water (in a small basin over some barely simmering water, or in the oven). Melt the butter and stir in the crumbled biscuits. Now line an 8-inch flan tin with an even layer of the biscuit mixture and pour over the bottom a coating of melted chocolate about ⅛ of an inch thick (don't attempt to spread the chocolate as it will disturb the biscuit base), and place in the refrigerator. Meanwhile, beat the cream cheese, sugar and concentrated orange to a smooth consistency, then spread it over the chocolate when it has hardened. Replace in the refrigerator and chill thoroughly before serving. (*Serves 8*)

White Horse Inn

Chilgrove, Sussex
East Marden 219

Nestling in a fold of the western edge of the Sussex downs, and commanding a village green all to itself, the White Horse has the most perfect setting an inn could wish (as regulars at Goodwood week know only too well). Three hundred years ago it was a humble farrier's and blacksmith's forge, where horses on the Chichester to Petersfield run could be serviced before tackling Harting Hill. Later a group of Chichester businessmen obviously concluded that passengers could do with a service as well, and added the present inn.

For the past four years Barry Phillips has been the keeper of this inn, and has built up a cellar of awesome range and character, supplementing it by frequent journeys to France (there are a hundred different clarets alone). The cooking is Adrian Congden's, who understandably doesn't attempt to compete with Mr Phillips' vintage ports at the end of a meal (so sweet dishes are not a speciality) but channels his skills into first and main courses. Between them, they are as formidable a combination as any you'll come across in these parts.

Fold all the ingredients very carefully into the mayonnaise, taste to check the seasoning, cover the dish and leave in a cool place for a couple of hours. Serve in individual portions on small crisp lettuce leaves garnished with sprigs of watercress and thin slices of cucumber and lemon. (*Serves 6 to 8*)

Pot Roasted Rabbit in Port Wine Sauce

Barry, the chef at the White Horse, suggests that the dregs of a bottle of vintage port would be especially nice for this.

1 wild rabbit
1 heaped tablespoon of seasoned flour
2 oz of butter
4 oz of unsmoked bacon (bought in one piece and cut into cubes)
4 oz of chopped onions
2 oz of button mushrooms (sliced)
1 bay leaf
1 clove of garlic
¾ pint of all-purpose stock (see page 152)
1 oz of flour and 1 oz of butter blended to make beurre manié
¼ pint of port
Salt, freshly milled black pepper

Pre-heat the oven to 375°F (mark 5).

Joint the rabbit into the 2 hind legs, 2 forelegs and a saddle. Dust the joints in seasoned flour. Melt the butter in a large frying pan and when frothy fry the rabbit joints on all sides to seal, then transfer them to a casserole. Now fry the onion, garlic, bacon and mushrooms for a few minutes and add them to the

rabbit, and throw in a bay leaf. Bring the stock to the boil; pour it in, followed by the port (through a strainer). Then put a lid on and bake in the oven until tender – about 1¼ hours. When cooked remove the rabbit, bacon and vegetables to a serving dish and keep warm, then boil up the sauce, adding small peanut-sized pieces of beurre manié to thicken. Taste to check the seasoning. Pour the sauce over the rabbit and serve. (*Serves 3; double the quantities for 6*)

Prawns Cheval Blanc

1 pint of freshly made mayonnaise (see page 151)
3 oz of shallots (finely chopped)
2 oz of celery (finely chopped)
2 oz of fresh peeled tomatoes (chopped small and with pips removed)
2 oz of double cream
1 level tablespoon of tomato purée
1 lb of fresh peeled prawns (squeezed to remove excess moisture)
Salt and freshly milled black pepper
Lettuce, watercress, cucumber and lemon

The Old House

Wickham, Hampshire
Wickham 3049

This old panelled house, fronting on to Wickham's attractive square, is certainly old enough (some three hundred years) and beautiful enough to be listed as a scheduled building. In 1970 it acquired a dining room – in what used to be the barn – which food inspectors and other discriminating palates have also found worth listing in their own way. Richard Skipwith, who runs the hotel, met his young French wife, who runs the kitchen, while he was working at Château Margaux. Clearly hospitality runs in the family. Her grandmother made a valuable collection of her own recipes, and in only two years the French provincial cooking that she produces here has brought the Old House high accolades – and that, without her repeating herself any single week.

Poires au Roquefort (or Stilton)

4 ripe dessert pears
2 oz of Roquefort (or Silton) cheese
½ to 1 oz of butter
3 to 4 tablespoons of cream cheese
A little single cream
Salt, paprika, freshly milled black pepper
A few lettuce leaves

Peel the pears, removing the core and pips from the centre, then cream the Roquefort cheese with the butter to the consistency of firm whipped cream and fill the middle of each pear with the mixture. Whisk a little single cream (or top of the milk) into the cream cheese till this mixture will just pour, then season it lightly. Place each pear on a lettuce leaf, coat with the cream cheese dressing and dust with paprika. Serve very cold with rolled brown bread and butter (or water biscuits). (*Serves 4*)

Cassoulet de Castelnaudary

1½ lb shoulder of mutton
3 level tablespoons of goose fat (or lard)
½ lb of garlic sausages
½ lb of fresh pork rind (scraped and cut into small pieces)
1 pig's hock
1¼ pints of beef consommé (you can use canned) or else good beef stock
½ lb of white beans (soaked overnight in cold water)
1 onion (stuck with a clove)
Bouquet garni
1 level tablespoon of tomato purée
Salt, freshly milled black pepper

Cut the shoulder of mutton into pieces (approx 1½ inches square) and brown them in the fat or lard in a large casserole. Add the sausages, pork rind and pig's hock, then cover and simmer for 20 minutes. Now add enough hot consommé to not quite cover the meats, replace the lid and continue to simmer over a low heat for 1 hour.
Cook the white beans together with the onion and bouquet garni in boiling salted water until the beans are half tender – about 30 minutes. Then drain them and add them to the meats, and season with a little salt and freshly milled black pepper. Cover and simmer gently for 1 further hour. After 30 minutes of the cooking time, add the tomato purée and check the seasoning. Serve in the same dish, very hot. (*Serves 4*)

Iced Orange Soufflé

For the orange ice:
6 navel oranges (medium-sized)
The grated rind of ½ an orange
1 fl. oz of lemon juice
6 oz of caster sugar
1 egg white (stiffly beaten)
1½ tablespoons of crystallised fruit (finely chopped)
1 dessertspoon of Grand Marnier

For the soufflé:
¼ pint of milk
2½ level tablespoons of caster sugar
2 oz of plain flour
1 level tablespoon of unsalted butter
2 egg yolks (lightly beaten)
3 egg whites (stiffly beaten)

Prepare the oranges by slicing the tops from them and scooping out the pulp, then squeeze all the juice from the pulps and strain, then add the lemon juice to the orange juice. Now dissolve the sugar in a cup of water, bring it to the boil and simmer for 5 minutes. Allow the mixture to cool and add it to the lemon/orange juice; add the grated orange rind, and freeze in the ice tray in the freezing compartment of the fridge (or in a churner freezer). When the mixture is half frozen, add the egg white to it and the chopped crystallised fruit mixed with the Grand Marnier. When it is completely frozen, pack each orange cup threequarters full with the ice, and keep cold.
Prepare soufflé. Dissolve sugar in milk and bring it to the boil. Mix flour to a paste with a little cold water, pour some of the hot milk into it and then add this mixture to the rest of the hot milk. Cook for 2 minutes, stirring all the time, then remove the saucepan from the heat, add the butter and egg yolks and fold in the egg whites. Pile the mixture into a piping bag and pipe it decoratively into the oranges and well above the rim. Cook in the oven (pre-heated to 350°F (mark 4)) until the top of the soufflé is golden – about 6 or 7 minutes. Serve immediately on a dish that allows the orange to sit upright. (*Serves 6*)

Horton Inn

Wimborne Minster, Dorset
Witchampton 252

Probably, since this locality is pitted with Roman roads and iron-age monuments, there has been habitation on this site from time immemorial. But this inn dates only from the late seventeenth century – though quite early enough for smugglers to have dragged their ill-gotten loot to it from Poole Flats. It lies on the estate of Lord Shaftesbury, whose ancestors built it, and who has now rebuilt it with the same attention to craftsmanship: you can't miss the coruscating Hicks décor, but unless you observed closely you might miss that the fine Yorkshire oak staircase is constructed, not with screws or nails, but with carved wedges of wood.

It is run by Captain and Mrs Lovelace with a comparable respect for the art of cooking, and the menus are appropriately aristocratic, having gained (in little more than five years) attention far beyond the limits of the Dorset downlands. And there is one singular advantage of being on His

Lordship's estate: whenever trout appears on the menu, you can be sure it has been plucked from the local trout stream by the estate officer himself only a few hours before.

Taramasalata

A smoked cod's roe paste.

1 lb of smoked cod's roe
2 slices of white bread (crusts off)
½ medium onion (grated)
1 fat clove of garlic (mashed)
4 tablespoons of olive oil
2 tablespoons of lemon juice
2 tablespoons of fresh chopped parsley
1 oz of green olives
A few crisp lettuce leaves

Scrape all the cod's roe from the skin, using a dessertspoon, and place it in a mortar. Trim the crusts off the bread, dip the bread in cold water, then squeeze all the water out and add the dampened bread to the cod's roe. Now pound the mixture to a smooth paste using a pestle and stir in the grated onion and the garlic. Add the olive oil and lemon juice, alternately in very small amounts, pounding well after each addition until it is all incorporated and the mixture takes on a smooth consistency. Press the mixture through a fine sieve. Serve the taramasalata piled onto crisp lettuce leaves, garnish with fresh chopped parsley and green olives. Eat with hot toast. (Note: if you don't have a pestle and mortar, a mixing bowl and wooden spoon are the next best thing.) (*Serves 8*)

Armenian Lamb Pilaff

2 lb of fillet end of leg of lamb
1 tablespoon of oil
1 oz of butter
2 onions (sliced)
1 clove of garlic (chopped)
1 level tablespoon of flour
1 level teaspoon of ground cumin seed
½ level teaspoon of ground allspice
2 level tablespoons of tomato purée
½ to ¾ pint of all-purpose stock (see page 152)
Salt, freshly milled black pepper

For the pilaff:
1½ oz of butter
1 small onion (finely chopped)
8½ oz of long-grain rice
¾ pint of chicken stock (see page 152)
Salt, freshly milled black pepper
3 oz of washed currants
3 oz of pistachio nuts (shredded)

Cut the meat from the bone and divide it into 2-inch squares. Heat the oil in a sauté pan, then add the butter and when it begins to foam brown the pieces of meat in it, a few at a time. Then, using a draining spoon, remove them to a casserole. Now add the onion and garlic to the pan and cook slowly for 5 minutes, stirring now and then. Sprinkle in the flour and spices, and cook for a further 3 to 4 minutes. Remove the pan from the heat then stir in the tomato purée and gradually add ½ pint of stock and blend till smooth. Now return the pan to the stove, bring to simmering point, then pour the contents of the pan over the meat in the casserole. Season with salt and pepper, put a lid on and bake in a pre-heated oven (350°F (mark 4)) for 45 minutes to 1 hour or until the meat is tender. Stir the mixture now and then during the cooking time, and if it needs it add a little more stock.

Meanwhile prepare the pilaff by melting two-thirds of the butter in a flameproof casserole, stir in the chopped onion and cook till soft and golden. Stir in the rice, cook for 2 to 3 minutes; pour in the stock, season and bring to the boil. Stir once more, cover and cook in the oven (same heat as above) for 20 to 25 minutes or until the rice is cooked and all the liquid is absorbed. Then add the rest of the butter, plus the currants and pistachio nuts.

Now arrange the meat etc in the middle of a serving dish, and keep warm. Reduce the liquid the meat was cooked in by boiling it (uncovered) on a fierce heat till reduced to a thick sauce, then pour over the meat, and pile the pilaff at either end of the serving dish. (*Serves 6*)

Crêpes Cappucino

1 standard batch of crêpes (see page 153 for batter)
3 oz of lightly toasted hazelnuts (chopped)

For the sauce:
½ lb of soft brown sugar
4 tablespoons of water
1 coffeecup of black coffee
2 tablespoons of Tia Maria liqueur
½ pint of whipped cream

First make the sauce by placing the sugar and water in a thick saucepan and bringing the mixture very slowly to the boil, stirring now and then. When it comes to the boil and the sugar has completely dissolved, turn the heat up and boil for about 2 or 3 minutes until the mixture has become dark and syrupy (don't overboil, or it will turn to toffee). Now stir in the coffee and Tia Maria to just heat through, and keep warm.

As you make the crêpes, sprinkle each one with chopped hazelnuts. Roll up and keep warm between two plates in a warm oven. To serve, pour the sauce all over the crêpes and decorate with piped whipped cream. (*Serves 6*)

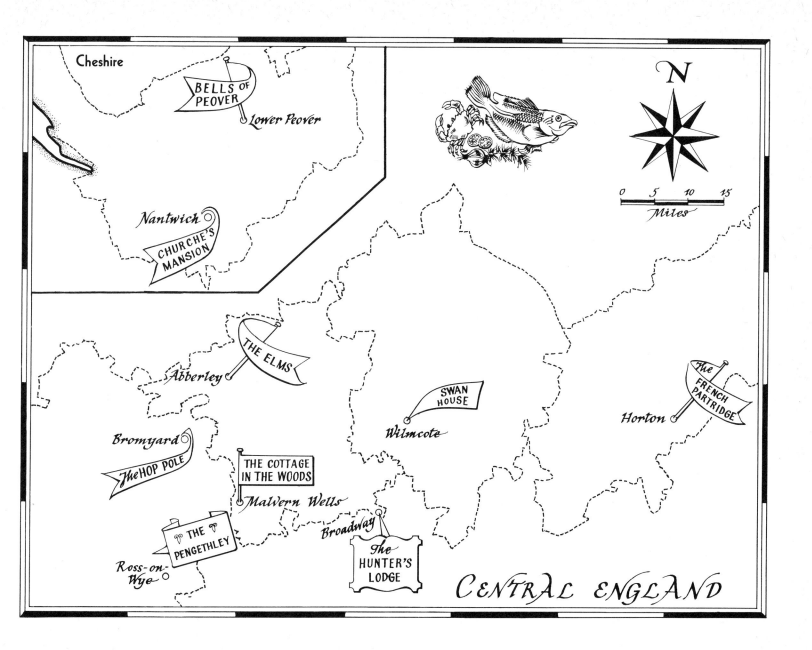

Cheshire

BELLS OF PEOVER

Lower Peover

Nantwich

CHURCHE'S MANSION

N

0 5 10 15
Miles

THE ELMS

Abberley

SWAN HOUSE

Wilmcote

The FRENCH PARTRIDGE

Horton

Bromyard

The HOP POLE

THE COTTAGE IN THE WOODS

Malvern Wells

Broadway

THE PENGETHLEY

Ross-on-Wye

The HUNTER'S LODGE

CENTRAL ENGLAND

The Hop Pole

Bromyard, Herefordshire
Bromyard 2449

There are any number of Hop Pole Inns in this neighbourhood to remind people that Hereford is one of Britain's largest hop-producing counties, but whereas most of them are devoted exclusively to the end product, the one in Bromyard has rather more to offer. It was once a noted coaching stop for this busy market town (and merited, we noticed, a mention in our ancient handbook of inns) but traces of that era are to be found round the back, rather than in the restrained Victorian front which looks out onto one of Bromyard's picturesque little squares. But what really distinguishes this Hop Pole from the rest of the field are Mr Bryan's menus, which invariably have something exciting to offer. Here, even the modest phrase 'assorted vegetables' conceals surprises and does no justice to the long procession of fresh plants from the kitchen-garden of England.

Salmon Trout Mousseline

1 salmon trout (1½ to 1¾ lb)
½ lb of cooked fresh salmon
2½ fl. oz of double cream
3 egg whites
3 bay leaves
1 lemon (cut into thin slices)
Salt, cayenne pepper

Pre-heat the oven to 350°F (mark 4).

Start by pounding the salmon until smooth, then gradually add the cream and season with a good pinch of cayenne pepper and salt. Beat the egg whites until they form soft peaks, then carefully fold them into the salmon mixture with a metal spoon. Clean the salmon trout and remove the backbone and any small fins, and season with salt and pepper. Now fill the cavity inside with the cream and salmon mixture, and wrap the fish up in well buttered foil, adding the bay leaves and lemon; pinch the edges together to seal well. Bake in a tray filled with just enough water to cover for 20 minutes in the oven. Allow to cool in the water, and don't unwrap and remove the skin until just before serving as this keeps it moist. (*Serves* 6)

Fillet of Pork with Apricots and Peppers

2 lb of pork fillet
2 green peppers
1 medium onion
4 oz of butter

For the sauce:
3 oz butter
3 oz flour
1½ pints of milk
1 medium tin of apricots (drained)
2 dessertspoons of made-up mustard
1 dessertspoon of Worcester sauce
Salt, freshly milled black pepper

Melt the butter in a thick-bottomed frying pan, slice the pork fillet into pieces ½ inch thick, and fry these in the butter until golden brown on both sides, then transfer them to a wide, shallow casserole. Now slice the peppers and onion finely, fry until tender in the remaining butter, then add them to the pork fillet. Make up a white sauce (with 3 oz of butter, 3 oz of flour to 1½ pints of milk) and season well. Finely chop (or blend) the apricots and add them to the sauce together with the mustard and Worcester sauce. Taste to check the seasoning. Pour over the pork fillet, cover with a lid or foil, and cook in a pre-heated oven (350°F (mark 4)) for 30 minutes. Serve with boiled rice. (*Serves* 6)

Malakoff Pudding

4 oz of ground almonds
4 oz of caster sugar
4 oz of butter
1 egg
½ oz of rum
2 oz of milk
¼ pint of whipped cream
A few glacé cherries

First cream the butter and sugar together until the mixture is very light and fluffy, then add the ground almonds and beat vigorously. Now add the egg, then the rum, and finally the milk, a little at a time, stirring continuously. Put this mixture into 6 individual moulds or dishes, and refrigerate well. Just before serving, dip the moulds into warm water, then turn out onto serving dishes, and decorate with whipped cream and glacé cherries. (*Serves* 6)

The Pengethley

Near Ross-on-Wye, Herefordshire
Harewood End 252

Good pheasant shooting, salmon fishing, beef rearing, strawberry growing country, this, and whoever first chose to build his country home here in Tudor times clearly had one eye on his table. His other eye was no doubt on the view, unspoiled even today, of very English fields and woods rolling away into the distance and the Welsh Marches.

Nothing remains of the Tudor house – though the Jacobean walled garden and stables escaped the fire (that is one theory anyway) and still stand today. In its place, in 1826, rose a spacious Georgian building, shuttered and white-walled, which for the past four years has been the realisation of Mr and Mrs Harvey's pipe-dream. Though, equally, one might say that such a house needed the Harveys – her elegant menus to grace the fine Georgian dining room, and his rare and distinguished wines to fill the Jacobean

cellars, for such combinations are unusual enough.

Chilled Cucumber Soup

2 medium cucumbers (peeled and sliced)
½ pint of natural yoghurt
¼ pint of soured cream
1 clove of garlic
Lemon juice to taste
1 teaspoon of finely chopped fresh mint
A little cold milk
Salt and freshly milled black pepper

Place the first four ingredients in a liquidiser (reserving a few paper-thin slices of cucumber for a garnish) and blend till smooth. If yours is a small liquidiser you may need to do this in two or three lots. Taste, and add a little lemon juice and some salt and freshly milled pepper. If the soup is a little too thick add some cold milk. Stir in the finely chopped mint, cover the bowl and chill thoroughly before serving. Serve each portion garnished with thinly sliced cucumber. (*Serves 4*)

Beef Trevarrick

2 lb of stewing steak
4 medium onions (finely chopped)
8 tomatoes (peeled and sliced)
2 cloves of garlic
7 fl. oz of sweet Vermouth
4 tablespoons of chopped parsley
Salt, freshly milled black pepper

Pre-heat the oven to 400°F (mark 6).

Trim the meat and cut it into 2-inch cubes, then butter an ovenproof casserole, arrange the meat, chopped onion and half the tomatoes in it, and add a seasoning of salt, freshly milled pepper and crushed garlic. Pour the Vermouth in, put a lid on and cook in the oven for 30 minutes. Have ready a roasting tin with about 2 inches of simmering water in it, then when the 30 minutes are up transfer the casserole to stand in the roasting tin of water. Now place the casserole (sitting in the tin of water) back in the oven, reduce the heat to 300°F (mark 2) and leave it there for a further 3 hours until the meat is tender enough to be cut with a fork. Just before serving arrange the rest of the sliced tomatoes over the meat and strew thickly with fresh chopped parsley. Serve hot. (*Serves 4*)

Banana Créole

The juice of 2 medium oranges
The juice of 1 lemon
1 dessertspoon of Grenadine syrup
1 level tablespoon of butter
1 level tablespoon of demerara sugar
4 bananas (peeled and sliced at an angle into ½-inch thick rounds)
2 tablespoons of rum
Whipped cream for decoration

First mix the orange and lemon juice with the Grenadine in a small basin. Then heat the butter and sugar together in a small saucepan until just melted. Add the sliced bananas and the fruit juice mixture, together with the rum, bring to simmering point and simmer until the liquid is reduced by half and the bananas are soft. Then taste and add more sugar and rum if you think it needs it. Divide the bananas and sauce between 4 serving dishes, top each one with whipped cream and serve immediately. (*Serves 4*)

The French Partridge

Horton, Northamptonshire
Hackleton 632

Horton is a tiny Northamptonshire village which stands soberly among a profusion of exotic-sounding neighbours like Buttock's Booth and Newton Blossomville. But Horton has one asset that the others don't – the French Partridge. No one knows quite how old the two component parts of the house are, but an ancient map shows clearly that both were in existence in 1622, one of them as an inn serving the busy London to Derby stage route. It flourished for another two hundred and fifty years until, predictably, the coming of the railways when, like so many others, it was pensioned off as a farm.

Now, a hundred years later, things have turned full circle; railways are bowing out to the car, and the road North is the M1. Drive a few miles east of it and you will find the inn at Horton, too, back in business, as a restaurant, and with a new name; Partridge, because that is the owners' name – and French because it was in a small family hotel near Toulouse that David Partridge learned to cook his delicious food which has been the envy of Easton Maudit and Yardley Gobion (indeed a great deal further afield) for the past ten years.

Smoked Haddock Coquilles

1 lb of finnan haddock (best quality)
½ pint of milk
1 oz of butter
1 oz of flour
Freshly milled white pepper
2 ½ fl. oz of cream
1 lb (approx) of creamed potatoes, with an egg beaten into the mixture
2 oz of grated cheese
6 well-buttered deep scallop shells

Poach the haddock in the milk in an oven at 350°F (mark 4) for 20 to 25 minutes. When cool, remove the haddock from the milk and flake it, removing all the skin and bones. Melt the butter, stir in the flour then add the strained milk in which the haddock was poached a little at a time, blending well after each addition until you have a smooth white sauce. Season only with freshly milled white pepper, as it's unlikely to need any salt. Now combine the flaked fish with the sauce and stir in the cream. Use the prepared potato to pipe a decorative border round the shells, then fill each shell with the fish, sprinkle with grated cheese and brown under a hot grill till golden and bubbling. (*Serves 6*)

Allumettes de Porc à la Crème

2 ½ lb of pork fillet (tenderloin) cut into large
    matchstick strips
½ lb of green peppers (de-pipped and sliced
    into matchsticks)
4 oz of mushrooms (sliced)
2 oz of onions (chopped)
2 oz of butter
¼ pint of white stock
½ pint of double cream
1 level teaspoon of arrowroot
Salt, freshly milled white pepper
½ teaspoon of ground ginger
Oil
½ pint of cider
Lemon juice
Croûtons

Sauté the onions in half the butter until soft;
add the sliced mushrooms and cook them
for 1 to 2 minutes. Mix the arrowroot with
a dessertspoon of cold water, and add it to
the stock which should then be poured over
the onions and mushrooms. Bring to simmering point and set on one side. Now melt
the other half of the butter in a separate pan
with a little oil and sauté the peppers until
soft. Remove them from the pan then quickly
sauté the pork, taking care not to overcook.
Now remove the pork, pour the cider and
the lemon juice into the pan and bubble at a
fierce heat until the mixture is reduced to
almost nothing. Next add the mushroom and
onion mixture to the pan, bring to simmering
point then add the pork, peppers, ginger and
seasoning, and finally the cream which should
be heated through without boiling. Serve
immediately with croûtons of fried bread.
(*Serves 6*)

Raspberry Meringue Baskets

These consist of basket-shaped meringue
cases with a little crème pâtisserie on the
bottom, and topped with fresh cream and
sugared raspberries (or other fruits in season).
The rims are decorated with piped fresh cream.

2 egg whites
4 oz of caster sugar
A pinch of salt
A few drops of lemon juice
Crème pâtisserie (see below)
Raspberries (or other fruit)
Whipped cream

First prepare a baking sheet by oiling it and
lining it with greaseproof paper, also oiled.
In a large clean bowl, whisk the egg whites,
salt and lemon juice until the mixture forms
soft peaks, then fold in the sugar. Pipe out
the bases of the small baskets onto the baking
sheet, using a star vegetable nozzle, and
increase the walls by further piping until the
basket shape is achieved. Place them in a
very cool oven 225°F (mark ¼) to dry out
for about 2 hours. Fill before serving. (*Serves 6*)

Crème Pâtisserie

1 pint of milk
2 eggs
2 extra egg yolks
2 oz of plain flour
3 oz of vanilla sugar (or ordinary sugar with
    2 drops of vanilla essence)

Heat the milk, and beat the eggs, flour and
sugar together, then strain this mixture into
the milk. Bring slowly to the boil, stirring all
the time and cook over a very low heat for
about 5 or 6 minutes. Then cool and chill
before using.

The Cottage in the Woods

Malvern Wells, Worcestershire
Malvern 3487

The cottage, to be truthful, is a large and handsome Georgian country house: and the woods are the profusely tree-lined and rhododendron-covered slopes of the Malvern hills looking out over the Vale of Evesham. As you drive up the twisting road to the hotel at night, the twinkling horizons of the plain expand before you. It was built originally as a dower house by a landed local family (related somehow by marriage to no less than the Duke of Gandolphi). It passed in due course to the Du Lapp sisters – noted patronesses of musicians in the days when Malvern was known as a Centre of the Arts as well as a watering-place. They built the music-room, much beloved by Elgar, and who knows what little pieces he may have composed here?

Michael Ross and his wife are the present owners, who found it a derelict guest house in 1965 and have transformed it into a place of style and elegance. If there is a Muse (as there should be) for cooking, she would surely stay here and approve highly of Mr Ross's compositions (to which Mrs Ross adds the sweet finales). And if ever there was an establishment where Malvern water was redundant, it is here where the Latours go back to 1934 and the malt whiskies take up several shelves.

Cream Cheese and Egg Mousse

½ pint of jellied consommé (this can be tinned)
8 oz of plain full-cream cheese
2 hard-boiled eggs
Salt, freshly milled black pepper

Slice the hard-boiled eggs and lay them in 4 individual moulds or ramekin dishes. Melt the consommé over a gentle heat and allow it to get almost cold. Mix the consommé into the cream cheese, gradually and thoroughly till very smooth. This can be done in a blender. Season to taste, then pour into the individual dishes, cover with foil and chill very thoroughly for 3 to 5 hours, or until set firm. Gently loosen the mousse round the edges, turn out onto individual serving dishes, and serve with cucumber salad. (*Serves 4*)

Chicken with Pernod

1 fresh frying chicken of best quality (cut into 8 small pieces; take the chicken liver as well)
¼ level teaspoon of powdered saffron
2 tablespoons of Pernod
8 tablespoons of olive oil
2 onions (chopped)
4 cloves of garlic (crushed)
6 tomatoes (peeled, seeded and chopped)
6 sprigs of parsley (chopped)
4 thickly sliced raw potatoes
4 slices of French bread
Salt, freshly milled black pepper

For the Sauce Rouille:
1 clove of garlic
4 small hot red peppers (de-seeded and chopped)
1½ fl. oz of olive oil
1 chicken liver
1 level tablespoon of butter

Place the chicken portions in a bowl, sprinkle them with saffron, salt and freshly milled black pepper, pour the Pernod and 5 tablespoons of olive oil over, and leave them to marinate for 30 minutes, turning them over once. Heat the remaining olive oil in a flameproof casserole and gently cook the onion and garlic till pale gold, then add the tomatoes and cook them for 5 minutes or so, stirring often. Now add the parsley, then the chicken pieces and the marinade. Cook the chicken pieces a little on all sides, then add enough water to almost cover the chicken (being careful not to add too much). Season with salt and freshly milled black pepper, cover and cook for 10 minutes. Now add the sliced

80

potatoes, cover again and cook for a further 15 minutes until the potatoes are nearly cooked through. Then uncover the cooking pot and let everything simmer and reduce for another 10 minutes or so (until the potatoes are completely cooked). Arrange 4 slices of French bread in the base of a serving dish, sprinkle with a little olive oil, pour the contents of the casserole over, and serve with the Sauce Rouille handed round separately.

For the sauce: sauté the chopped chicken liver in a little butter very quickly, and lightly mash it with a fork. In a blender, blend the garlic, chopped pepper and olive oil till smooth, add the chicken liver, blend again then finally add 2 slices of potato from the casserole and 6 tablespoons of casserole sauce. Blend till smooth. Reheat the sauce, pour it in a bowl and serve separately. (*Serves 6*)

Fudge and Walnut Pie

1 prepared 8- or 9-inch round pastry case
4 oz of good quality walnut halves (roughly chopped)
10 oz of white sugar
10 oz of soft brown sugar
1 pinch of salt
4 level tablespoons of butter
2 teaspoons of vanilla essence
8 fl. oz of single cream

Place both sugars and the cream in a thick saucepan, bring slowly to the boil, and when the sugar has dissolved, boil the mixture until a drop of it forms a soft ball when plunged into ice-cold water. (If you have a cooking thermometer, you'll find the mixture will reach this stage at 240°.) Remove the saucepan from the heat, add salt, butter and vanilla essence without stirring, then allow the mixture to cool down to lukewarm; beat it to a creamy consistency. Stir the walnuts into the mixture, and pour it into the pastry case. Serve with whipped cream. (*Serves 4*)

The Elms

Abberley, Worcestershire
Great Witley 231

As you drive up the long, grand driveway to the Elms, it's almost as if you've been invited out to dinner at some stately home, and the magnificent façade of this Queen Anne mansion looming up ahead

does nothing to dispel the illusion. The core of it was built by a pupil of Sir Christopher Wren, Gilbert White (who also built the Guildhall in Worcester); the wings were added later. In fact the shell of the building (apart from the formal gardens) is all that remains of its former glory, for earlier this century it was completely gutted by fire. All the

same, the interior is handsomely restored – not unlike a cosy London club with deep armchairs, panelled bar and roaring open fires.

In any other circumstances such surroundings might well eclipse the food, but Mrs Schadler is the chef here and has seen to it that they don't. Her cooking has won acclaim for the best part of twenty years now, and we can vouch for the fact that her famous Chocolate Orange Mousse has lost absolutely nothing with the passage of time.

Peaches in Curry Cream Sauce

4 fresh peaches (peeled and cut in halves or sliced)

For the sauce:
2 level dessertspoons of curry powder
1 level dessertspoon of ground ginger
1 pinch of salt
4 tablespoons of apple jelly (or apricot jam)
2 ½ fl. oz of port (or Marsala)
¼ pint of fresh cream

Mix all the sauce ingredients together quite thoroughly, then press the mixture through a fine sieve. Arrange the peaches in 4 individual serving dishes, pour the sauce over and chill before serving. (*Serves 4*)

Escalope of Veal with Anchovy Sauce

4 escalopes of veal (4–6 oz each)
1 oz of flour
2 oz of butter
2 tablespoons of oil
8 anchovy fillets (pounded to paste)
¼ pint of soured cream
¼ pint of strong all-purpose stock (see page 152)
Salt, freshly milled black pepper, paprika

Season the escalopes with salt and freshly milled black pepper and dip each one in flour. In a heavy frying pan melt the butter together with 2 tablespoons of oil, and sauté the escalopes for 4 or 5 minutes on each side until they are golden brown and tender. Then transfer them to a serving dish and keep warm. To make the sauce, pour off almost all the fat from the pan, leaving only a thin film on the bottom and sides of the pan. Pour in the veal stock and boil briskly for a few minutes, stirring continuously. Add the pounded anchovy fillets, a pinch of paprika and the cream, then stir till the mixture is smooth. When the sauce has reduced and has the consistency of thick cream, taste to check the seasoning, then pour over the escalopes. Serve at once. (*Serves 4*)

Chocolate Orange Mousse

7 oz of plain chocolate
3 whole eggs
2 eggs (separated)
3 oz of caster sugar
1 orange (grated rind and juice)
2 fl. oz of water
½ oz of powdered gelatine
3 fl. oz of double cream (whipped lightly)

For the decoration:
¼ pint of double cream (whipped)
4 orange segments
A little grated chocolate

Soak the powdered gelatine in the orange juice (in an old cup) then stand it in a pan of barely simmering water until it has dissolved and is quite transparent. Meanwhile place the

egg yolks, whole eggs and sugar in a basin fitted over a pan of simmering water, and whisk with an electric whisk until the mixture is thick and creamy. Remove the basin from the heat, then put another basin over the simmering water containing the broken-up chocolate and water and leave it to melt.

When the chocolate has melted, stir till smooth, add the grated orange rind and, when it has cooled, stir it into the egg mixture. Now pour the melted gelatine through a strainer into the mixture, mix thoroughly and when the mixture is just at the point of setting, carefully fold in the lightly whipped cream and the stiffly beaten egg whites. Pour the mixture into a soufflé dish, cover and chill till firm (about 3 hours). Decorate with whirls of whipped cream, orange segments and grated chocolate. (*Serves 4*)

The Hunters Lodge

Broadway, Worcestershire
Broadway 3247

Broadway is the showplace of the Cotswolds: each side of its long and wide main thoroughfare is a set-piece of elegant Cotswold houses, idyllic cottages, inns, blossoming gardens. It all depends on what you come to Broadway to find. If it is history in golden stone, you might be forgiven for not making for the Hunters Lodge, discreetly tucked back from the road (though there is history enough in this Cromwellian manor house). But if it is for fine food and wine, this is where to come. It was here, three Easters ago, after lashings of Huntsman's Pie, that this book began to germinate: the peaceful countryside, the enthusiasm of the cooking, the splendid fire – but we have explained all this at the beginning. When we returned this Easter, the enthusiasm had not dimmed, and the herbs grew as abundantly in the garden. Mrs Reynolds' staff is young, adventurous and inventive (mailing lists frequently announce an impending special 'national' evening). Broadway doesn't change, but Mrs Reynolds' menus do with dizzying speed, constantly drawing you back.

84

Baked Avocado with Walnut Butter

2 small avocados
2 oz of chopped walnuts
2 oz of butter

8 lean rashers of bacon
Freshly milled black pepper

Pre-heat the oven to 375°F (mark 5).

Mix the walnuts with the butter, then halve the avocados, remove the stones and then the skins. Season the avocados with freshly milled black pepper, stuff the cavities with walnut butter and wrap each one with 2 rashers of bacon. Place them all in a foil-lined roasting tin and bake for 15 to 20 minutes or until the bacon is crisp and the avocados soft. Serve immediately with lots of fresh crusty bread. (*Serves 4*)

Filet de Boeuf en Chemise

4 fillet steaks
¾ lb of puff pastry
1 medium onion (cut into rings)
2 cloves of garlic
1 small lemon (cut into thin slices)
2 teaspoons of fresh chopped thyme
4 bay leaves
3 to 4 oz of butter
1 egg yolk
Salt, freshly milled black pepper

Sear the steaks on both sides in a little butter and allow to cool. Roll out the pastry quite thin, cut it into 4 squares, and place a cooled fillet on the centre of each piece of pastry. Then season with salt and freshly milled black pepper. In a frying pan fry the onion rings and crushed garlic gently in butter, add the lemon slices and a seasoning of thyme and 4 bay leaves. Cook for a minute or two, then remove from the heat and allow to cool. Pre-heat the oven to 425°F (mark 7). Divide the cooled mixture over each fillet (retaining the juices left in the pan), then dampen the edges of the pastry and bring all 4 corners together at the top, sealing well. Now place each parcel on a baking sheet, brush with beaten egg yolk and bake for 20 to 25 minutes until the pastry is cooked. Melt some more butter with the juices left in the pan and cook till brown (beurre noir), pour over the fillets and serve. (*Serves 4*)

Grapes in Cointreau Custard

8 oz of large firm white grapes (halved, peeled and pipped)
1 miniature bottle of Cointreau (or 4 table-spoons)

For the custard:
6 large egg yolks
1 pint of double cream
2 oz of caster sugar
3 or 4 drops of vanilla essence

To decorate:
¼ pint of whipped cream
2 oz of peeled, halved and pipped grapes

Place the prepared grapes in a dish, sprinkle the Cointreau over, cover and chill for a few hours. To make custard, beat the egg yolks, add the sugar, heat the cream till very hot, and pour it over the egg yolks. Add a few drops of vanilla essence, then pour the mixture back into a double saucepan (or a basin fitted over a saucepan of barely simmering water), and continue stirring until the custard has thickened, then remove from the heat and cool slightly. Arrange the grapes and juice in 6 individual ramekin dishes, pour the cooled custard over, cover and chill again for a minimum of 2 hours. Serve decorated with blobs of whipped cream and halved, peeled grapes. (*Serves 6*)

Bells of Peover

Lower Peover, near Knutsford, Cheshire
Lower Peover 2269

The bells have, in fact, nothing to do with the adjacent timbered church of St Oswald, which together with the inn and its outbuildings make up a picturesque and very ancient cluster in this otherwise scattered village. Bell was a former landlord, long since dead, and the apostrophe seems to have died with him. But the inn does have connections with the church, for it was on this site that the curate and sacristan lived in the thirteenth century (and in honour of the association, in 1969 Bells celebrated the seventh centenary of St Oswald's by roasting a whole ox in the courtyard).

There has been an inn here since the middle of the sixteenth century, owned by the Leycesters of Tabley whose crest still adorns the north gable: even within living memory it was called the Warren de Tabley Arms. There are, no doubt, veterans in America who still remember it as one of General Patten's more congenial headquarters. But most people nowadays will remember it for the food from Mr Goodier-Fisher's kitchen, generous, fresh and admirably cooked; for the fresh local cheese, and the vegetables delivered post-haste from a parishioner's garden.

Mussels Breton

3 quarts of prepared mussels (see page 153)
1 stick of celery (chopped)
1 medium onion (chopped)
1 pint of water

For the garlic butter:
6 oz of butter (room temperature)
1 oz of breadcrumbs
1 heaped teaspoon of fresh chopped parsley
1 clove of garlic (crushed)
The juice of a small lemon

First make the garlic butter by blending all the ingredients thoroughly together. Then place the mussels (cleaned) in a large pan together with the onion, celery and a pint of water, put a lid on and steam them open over a fierce heat, shaking the pan now and then. Allow the mussels to cool; retain the mussels still clinging to their half shells and replace any loose mussels in their shells – discard all the empty half shells. Heat the oven to 450°F (mark 8), place the mussels in 6 individual heatproof dishes, cover each one with a blob of garlic butter, and bake in the oven for about 10 to 15 minutes, or until the butter is sizzling noisily. Serve at once with lots of crusty bread to mop up the delicious juices. (*Serves 6*)

Beefsteak and Cowheel Pie

½ lb of shortcrust pastry
2 lb of stewing steak (cut into smallish cubes)
½ cowheel (cut into 1-inch pieces)
¼ pint of stock
1 large onion (chopped)
2 oz of mushrooms (chopped)
1 oz of beef dripping
1 oz of plain flour
Salt, freshly milled black pepper

Pre-heat the oven to 425°F (mark 7).

Melt the dripping in a saucepan and fry the onion and mushrooms in it for about 6 minutes, then add the stewing steak. Brown it on all sides, then sprinkle in the flour and stir it round to soak up the juices. Next add the pieces of cowheel, and gradually stir in the stock and seasoning. Pour into a suitably-sized pie dish, cover with shortcrust pastry, and bake in a hot oven for 10 minutes. Then reduce the heat to 300°F (mark 2) and cook further for about 2 hours. (*Serves 6*)

Blackberry and Apple Meringue

1 7-inch round of Genoese sponge, (see Baked Alaska, page 117)
2 cooking apples (stewed)
2 lb of blackberries (fresh or frozen)
A little jam and caster sugar

For the meringue:
4 large egg whites
8 oz of caster sugar
A pinch of salt

Pre-heat the oven to 425°F (mark 7).

Place the sponge on an ovenproof plate, spread it with jam and with the stewed apple. Heap on the blackberries, doing the best you can to form a pyramid shape, then sprinkle with caster sugar. Beat the egg whites with a pinch of salt till stiff, then beat in the caster sugar a little at a time, beating well after each addition. Cover the blackberries and the sponge completely with the meringue mixture and bake in a hot oven for about 5 minutes, and serve at once. (*Serves 4 to 6*)

Churche's Mansion

Nantwich, Cheshire
Nantwich 65933

Nantwich, whose commercial prosperity was once based on salt, has had a remarkable history of royal connections, from Offa onwards. Elizabeth I helped to rescue it after a disastrous fire; Charles II tried, with little success, to fine it for its Parliamentary sympathies. Churche's Mansion, built in 1577 by Richard Churche, one of the town's many notable merchants, has seen it all – the Hanoverian window-tax which deprived it of ten windows, Victorian negligence which allowed it to fall into decrepitude as a storehouse and, little better, as a Young Girls' Boarding School, and enlightened concern in the twentieth century, which has restored it to much of its former glory.

This concern came from a doctor and his wife who, in spite of local apathy, rescued the building from being shipped timber by timber across the Atlantic in 1931. Over the next twenty-five years they restored and rehabilitated this glorious house with its Tudor timbers, windows, hearths and even the initials of Richard Churche and his wife Marjorie. Today, under the next generation of Myotts, it houses a restaurant of distinction using produce as genuine as the house itself. Even the butter is from the local farm, and

Mrs Clowes, the cook here for twenty years, opened a veritable vaultful of home-made cakes for our inspection. Mrs Curzon, after a mere seventeen years, now cooks the dinners, perpetuating the new tradition – of fine food – at Churche's Mansion.

Chicken Véronique

1 4-lb chicken and giblets
½ pint of chicken stock (see page 152)
4 oz of butter
1 dessertspoon of fresh, chopped tarragon (or ½ teaspoon if dried)
1 dessertspoon of fresh, chopped marjoram (or ½ teaspoon if dried)
4 fl. oz of dry white wine
1 level teaspoon of cornflour
3 tablespoons of double cream
4 oz of white grapes (skinned, halved and de-pipped)
Salt, freshly milled black pepper

Pre-heat the oven to 425°F (mark 7).

Make the chicken stock from the giblets, as directed on page 152. Mix a tablespoon of butter with the herbs in a small basin, adding a good seasoning of salt and freshly milled black pepper. Then place this mixture inside the chicken, truss it, and rub the rest of the butter all over the outside of the bird. Place it breast side up in a roasting tin in the oven, then after 10 minutes turn the chicken on to its side, reduce the heat to 350°F (mark 4), baste well, then cook it for 30 minutes. Turn it onto the other side, baste again and cook for a further 30 minutes. Now lift the chicken out of the tin, drain well, carve, cover with foil and keep warm.

To make the sauce, skim the fat from the roasting pan, then add the wine to the remaining juices and boil briskly, stirring around till the juices are reduced by half. Pour in the chicken stock, let it bubble for a minute, then add the cornflour blended till smooth with a tablespoon of cold water. Bring to the boil again, stirring, simmer for 5 minutes, then turn the heat right down. Stir in the cream and the grapes, taste to check seasoning, then spoon the sauce over the chicken and serve immediately. (*Serves 4*)

Iced Damson Soufflé

2 lb of damsons (fresh or frozen)
6 oz of caster sugar
¾ pint of double cream (lightly whipped)
3 egg whites

Put the damsons in a large saucepan with ¼ pint of water and the sugar. Bring to the boil and cook gently, uncovered, for about 10 minutes or until the damsons are soft and pulpy. Have ready a large sieve over an equally large bowl, and pour the contents of the saucepan into the sieve, then leave it to drain until all the cooking liquid has drained away. Reserve the syrup in the bowl and then place the sieve over another bowl and rub the damsons through, extracting all the stones. Then when it's quite cold, carefully fold the lightly whipped cream into the damson purée. Now whisk the egg whites till stiff and fold them carefully into the mixture. Pour the mixture into 6 stemmed glasses or ramekin dishes. Cover and chill for at least 3 or 4 hours. Just before serving spoon the remaining damson syrup over the top of each portion. (*Serves 6*)

Swan House

Wilmcote, Warwickshire
Stratford-upon-Avon 2030

If, as we did, you arrive in Wilmcote with a little time to kill, what better than a stroll down the road to look round Mary Arden's cottage and work up an appetite? Shakespeare's mother certainly had a handsome home – more a large thatched house than a cottage – but a miniscule kitchen. Still, the butter churns and other implements in the rural museum outside demonstrate the bard wasn't reared on convenience foods.

Mr Stuart Parson's Swan House, a hundred yards away, would never dream of using convenience foods either, even if its kitchens are rather more automated and efficient. Two young girls, Jenny Burton and Sue Rea, are in charge of them and every three weeks dream up a long, new and exciting menu. Their cooking has won them nearly every major food award going – and they look (indeed they are) so *young*. One wonders what greater heights their cooking will achieve when they've got a few more years behind them. Give us excess of it, as Shakespeare might have said.

Cream Cheese Soup with Cheese Profiteroles

3 pints of milk
3 oz of butter
3 oz of plain flour
½ lb Cheddar cheese (finely grated)
Salt and freshly milled black pepper

For the choux pastry:
¼ pint of water
2 oz of margarine
3 oz of plain flour
1 pinch of salt
1 egg
2 oz of cream cheese (for the filling)

Pre-heat the oven to 400°F (mark 6).

First make the choux pastry by melting the margarine in the water in a saucepan over a medium heat. When the margarine has melted shake in the sifted flour and salt all at once, then beat vigorously until the mixture leaves the side of the pan. Remove from the heat and allow it to cool slightly – when cool beat in the egg until smooth. Turn the mixture into a nylon forcing bag with a ½-inch plain round nozzle and pipe small ½-inch blobs of paste on to a greased baking sheet, and bake for 12 to 15 minutes or until golden brown, then cool on a wire rack.

To make the soup, gently melt the butter in a heavy-based saucepan, stir in the flour till smooth, then start to add the milk gradually, beating well after each addition. When all the milk is in bring to simmering point and simmer very gently for 5 minutes. Then remove the saucepan from the heat and beat in the grated cheese, and season to taste with salt and freshly milled black pepper. All this can be done well in advance. To serve the soup, re-heat gently, split the tiny choux buns and fill each one with cream cheese, then serve the soup piping hot garnished with the profiteroles. (*Serves 8*)

Kidneys Bourguignonne

1 lb of button mushrooms (wiped)
1 lb of button onions (peeled)
1 pint of stock (homemade or a cube)
½ pint of red wine
3 oz of dripping
3 oz of plain flour
Freshly chopped parsley and croûtons (see page 153) for garnishing
3½ lb of lamb's kidneys (approx 3 per person)

For the forcemeat:
6 oz of fresh white breadcrumbs
4 oz of pork sausage meat
2 teaspoons freshly chopped mixed herbs (or 2 level teaspoons dried)
Salt and freshly milled black pepper

First make the forcemeat by mixing the sausage meat, fresh white breadcrumbs, herbs and seasonings – no liquid is added because the mixture has to be very stiff to remain inside the kidneys whilst cooking. Prepare the kidneys by taking off the skins and snipping out the white cores with a pair of scissors. Pack a small amount of forcemeat into each kidney interior where the core has been cut out.

To prepare the sauce melt the dripping in a large flameproof casserole, stir in the flour

and cook it to a rich brown colour. Add the stock bit by bit, stirring until smooth after each addition, add the wine and a seasoning of salt and freshly milled black pepper. Next carefully place the stuffed kidneys into the sauce, then add the onions and mushrooms. Put a lid on and cook in the oven at 325°F (mark 3) for 2½ to 3 hours or until tender. Serve with a sprinkling of freshly chopped parsley and crisp fried croûtons. (*Serves 8*)

Apple and Hazelnut Galette

3 oz of hazelnuts
3 oz of butter (room temperature)
2 rounded tablespoons of caster sugar
4½ oz of plain flour
1 pinch of salt

For the filling:
1 lb of dessert apples
Grated rind of 1 lemon and 1 orange
2 tablespoons of sultanas
2 tablespoons of currants
¼ level teaspoon of mixed spice
1 level dessertspoon of icing sugar
¼ pint of double cream (lightly whipped)

First prepare the galette by setting aside 8 whole hazelnuts and blending the rest till finely chopped – if you don't have an electric blender or grinder you can either put the nuts through a mincer or simply chop them very finely. In a mixing bowl whip the butter to soften it, then beat in the sugar till light and fluffy. Stir in the sifted flour and salt and finally the hazelnuts. When everything is thoroughly combined cover the bowl and

91

chill the mixture for at least 30 minutes. While that's happening, peel and slice the apples, put them into a thick saucepan with the orange and lemon rind, sultanas, currants and mixed spice, and let them soften over a very low heat – don't add any liquid but shake the pan from time to time to prevent them sticking.

Pre-heat the oven to 375°F (mark 5).

Divide the chilled mixture in two, and press each half into a 9-inch round shallow sandwich or flan tin, pressing the mixture evenly all over the base. Place the tins in the pre-heated oven and bake for about 10 minutes, then cool slightly and cut one round into 8 portions. When completely cool, turn out the complete round onto a serving plate, spread the apple mixture all over, then arrange the cut sections on top and dredge with icing sugar. Pipe 8 rosettes of whipped cream on top and decorate them with the whole hazelnuts. (*Serves 8*)

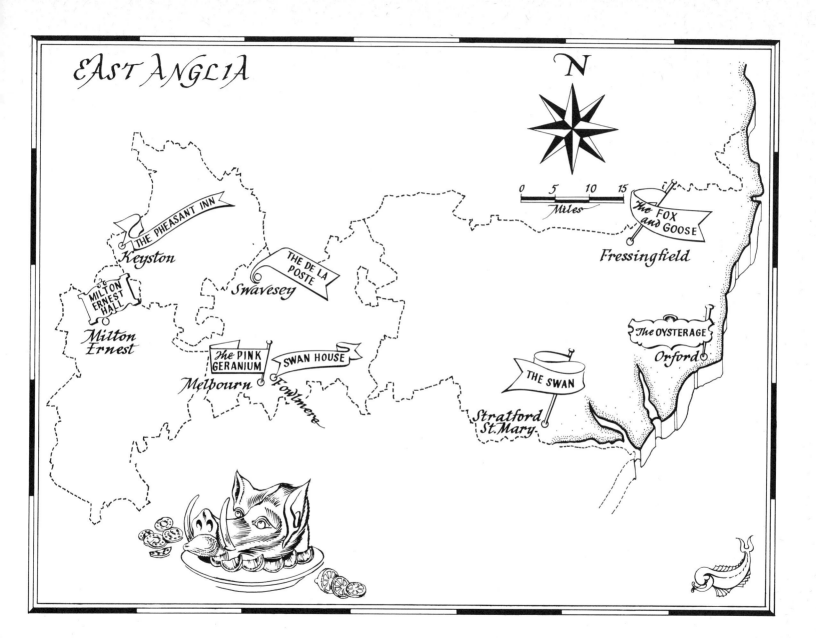

EAST ANGLIA

N

0 5 10 15
Miles

THE PHEASANT INN
Keyston

MILTON ERNEST HALL

Milton Ernest

THE DE LA POSTE
Swavesey

The PINK GERANIUM   SWAN HOUSE
Melbourn   Fowlmere

The FOX and GOOSE
Fressingfield

The OYSTERAGE
Orford

THE SWAN
Stratford St. Mary

Milton Ernest Hall

Milton Ernest, Bedfordshire
Oakley 4111

By the side of the River Ouse stands the one and only stately home designed by the famous Victorian architect William Butterfield. If the abuse heaped upon Keble College in Oxford by generations of undergraduates has been his undoing, surely the growing fame of Milton Ernest Hall will be his renaissance. It is a magnificent neo-Gothic edifice, romantic and elegant, a testament to Victorian spaciousness (so spacious, in fact, that the first owner in 1854 went broke trying to live in it). It could not quite accommodate the entire United States Eighth Army's air force, but it did supply a roof to Glen Miller before his fateful flight and (if you recall the film) it was where he gave his poignant concert.

The owners for the past two years, the Harmer-Browns, have an unashamed feeling for the old place, and have reverently restored it to a remarkable degree of homely comfort as a hotel. Equally important, perhaps, they have galvanised the acres of kitchen into creative activity. The food is memorable, not to say regal. And where else could you retire to a Conservatory to sip your brandy under the moonlight?

Terrine du Chef

1 lb of chicken livers
4 oz of lean pork
4 oz of raw boned chicken
2 oz of streaky bacon (chopped)
½ lb of long back bacon (unsmoked)
2 oz of butter
1 onion (chopped small)
2 cloves of garlic (crushed)
1 oz of pine nuts (available from wholefood shops)
2 fl. oz of brandy
1 pinch of dried tarragon
1 tablespoon of chopped parsley
12 juniper berries
6 bay leaves
Salt, freshly milled black pepper

Pre-heat the oven to 250°F (mark ½).

Sauté the finely chopped onion and streaky bacon in the butter with the crushed garlic for 5 minutes or so, then add the chicken livers, 2 bay leaves, a pinch of tarragon, a good seasoning of coarsely ground black pepper and not quire a flat teaspoon of salt. When the livers are cooked, pour in the brandy to moisten, remove the pan from the heat, extract the bay leaves, and when the mixture is cool enough pass it all through the coarse blade of the mincer. Cut the raw chicken and pork into small dice and add them to the mixture with the pine kernels and 8 juniper berries (crushed with the back of a tablespoon). Now add the chopped parsley, and mix everything very thoroughly. Line an oblong terrine dish with strips of long back bacon, allowing them to overlap at the edges. Now press the mixture into this and fold the overlapping bacon over the surface. Garnish with the rest of the bay leaves and juniper berries. Stand the terrine in a baking tin half-filled with hot water, place in the centre of the oven and cook it for 2 to 3 hours. (*Serves 8 to 10*)

Pork Fillet Stuffed with Walnuts, Prunes and Almonds with a white wine sauce

2 whole pork fillets

For the stuffing:
6 oz of prunes (covered and soaked overnight in dry white wine)
8 oz of good pork sausage meat
6 oz of ground almonds
4 oz of walnut halves
1 egg (beaten)
Salt, freshly milled black pepper

Softened butter

For the sauce:
1 oz of butter
1 oz of plain flour
¼ pint of dry white wine
4 tablespoons of double cream

Pre-heat the oven to 375°F (mark 5).

Take a sharp knife and split the pork fillets in half lengthways, then with a rolling pin batter them all the way down each length to flatten. Drain the prunes, halve them, take out the stones, and put them in a mixing bowl with the sausage meat, ground almonds and walnut halves. Add the beaten egg then mix

roasting tin and bake for about 40 minutes or until tender.

Towards the end of the cooking time, prepare the sauce by melting the butter in a small saucepan, stirring in the flour and gradually adding the wine a little at a time. Stirring constantly, cook the sauce very gently for about 8 minutes and then stir in the double cream. When the meat is cooked and transferred into a warm serving dish, spoon off all the fat from the juices and add a little of these cooking juices to the sauce. Adjust the seasoning and serve at once. (*Serves 6*)

Fresh Peach and Banana Pudding

4 large bananas (not over-ripe)
4 large eggs (separated)
1 pint of double cream
1 level dessertspoon of caster sugar
3 medium firm ripe peaches (peeled and sliced)
2 oz of lightly toasted flaked almonds

Put the peeled bananas in a large mixing bowl, add the yolks of the eggs and the sugar, and mash with a fork to combine everything evenly. Then whip the cream till stiff and carefully fold half of it into the banana mixture. Now whip the egg whites till stiff and fold them into the remainder of the cream. Arrange the sliced peaches over the base of a serving dish, and add the banana mixture, smoothing it evenly, followed by the egg white and cream mixture. Sprinkle the lightly toasted flaked almonds all over the surface, cover and chill thoroughly before serving. (*Serves 6*)

everything together very thoroughly – adding a seasoning of salt and freshly milled black pepper. Now spread the mixture over 2 of the flattened fillets, then replace the other 2 fillets on top, and tie into a neat shape in several places with string. Rub the meat all over with the softened butter and season with salt and pepper. Place the fillets in a

The Swan

Stratford St Mary, Suffolk
Dedham 2164

With the river Stour flowing virtually past its doorstep, this Ind Coope inn is deep in the Constable country (indeed the odds are that it was at the Swan that the painter would have caught the stage for his momentous journey to London early in his career). Not a lot has changed along this edge of Suffolk since the days when flocks of Norfolk turkeys were to be seen (according to Defoe) being ceremoniously marched in easy stages to London for the Christmas slaughter. The vast pens which housed them overnight have disappeared from the back of the Swan, but Constable's familiar landscapes are still fairly familiar and unspoiled.

The inn even has royal associations: George II is known to have 'reclined' here for a few hours after a gruelling reception at Lowestoft on his return from Germany. He did not eat anything then – which doubtless saved the poor innkeeper a few pennies – but he probably couldn't have resisted it if Marjorie and Alan Lloyd had been in residence at the time. At the very least he would have had one of their delicious snacks at the bar: better still, he would have tarried awhile for a meal in the charming little restaurant, and waited while his peas and beans were hand-picked from the garden (which has been known to happen).

Kitchen Garden Soup

1 lb of leeks (cleaned and chopped)
4 celery stalks (chopped small)
¾ lb of carrots (cleaned and thinly sliced)
¾ lb of courgettes (sliced, skins left on)
1 Spanish onion (peeled and chopped small)
4 oz of streaky bacon (rinds off)
2 tablespoons of olive oil
2 oz of butter
1 fat clove of garlic (crushed)
3 pints of chicken stock (can be made from a cube)
1 level tablespoon of tomato purée
Salt, freshly milled black pepper
2 tablespoons of chopped parsley)

Prepare all the vegetables as directed above, then start by melting the butter and oil in a large thick-bottomed saucepan. Add the bacon, cut into small pieces; fry it gently until the fat runs, then add all the prepared chopped vegetables and garlic. Stir them round and round till they're all glistening and

buttery, then – keeping the heat low – put a lid on the saucepan and let them 'sweat' for 15 to 20 minutes, stirring now and then. Pour the stock in, season with a little salt and some freshly milled black pepper, then simmer very gently for 2 hours without a lid. Just before serving, stir in the tomato purée and fresh chopped parsley, and taste to check the seasoning. (*Serves 6 to 8*)

Chicken Mexicana

12 chicken drumsticks
½ pint of dry white wine
Salt and freshly milled black pepper

For the sauce:
2 level tablespoons of butter
1 large green pepper (seeded and chopped)
1 large red pepper (seeded and chopped)
2 medium onions (roughly chopped)
1 fat clove of garlic (crushed)
4 oz of button mushrooms (thinly sliced)
2 level tablespoons of tomato purée
2 level teaspoons of cornflour
2 level teaspoons of demerara sugar
Salt and freshly milled black pepper
Savoury rice (see Pilaff, page 71)

Place the chicken in a casserole large enough to take all the drumsticks in a single layer, season with freshly milled black pepper and salt, then pour in the wine and ½ pint of water. Bring to the boil and simmer gently for 25 to 30 minutes or until the chicken is tender. While this is happening, heat 2 level tablespoons of butter in a saucepan, add the onions, chopped peppers and crushed garlic, and cook gently for 10 minutes, stirring now

and then. Next add the mushrooms, cook for a further 10 minutes, then stir in the tomato purée, and keep the heat very low. Now strain the chicken joints, reserving the cooking liquid, and remove all the meat from the bones, discarding the skin. In a small saucepan fast boil the cooking liquid till reduced to ¾ pint, then stir it into the vegetable mixture; blend the cornflour with a tablespoon of water and blend that in as well. Bring to simmering point, add the sugar, taste to check seasoning, and finally add the chicken pieces, let them gently heat through and serve piled onto a bed of pilaff rice. (*Serves 6*)

Caramel Meringue Glacé

Caramel sauce (see page 152)
A family size block of vanilla icecream

For the meringues:
2 egg whites
4 oz of caster sugar

Pre-heat the oven to 260°F (mark ½).

Prepare a baking sheet by lining it with grease-proof paper and brushing it with oil, or use non-stick parchment. Put the egg whites in a clean grease-free bowl, then using a clean dry whisk beat them till they stand in stiff peaks. Now whisk in the caster sugar, about 1 dessertspoon at a time. When all the sugar is whisked in, use a tablespoon and spoon 12 individual blobs of meringue onto the oiled tin. Place the baking sheet in the oven (lowest shelf) and let the meringues dry out for 1 hour. Leave them in the oven either overnight or until the oven is completely cold again, then carefully remove them from the baking tin and store in an airtight tin till needed. To serve sandwich the meringues (2 per person) together with vanilla ice cream, pour the caramel sauce over them and serve immediately. (*Serves 6*)

The Fox and Goose

Fressingfield, near Diss, Norfolk
Fressingfield 247

The guide books to Fressingfield will draw your attention to the fine Flemish weavers' church and gloat over its fifteenth-century pew-ends. But further up the hill there is a mellow timbered inn, edging itself almost into the church-yard, and the truth is that it's food, not pew-ends, that brings most pilgrims to Fressingfield. For Mr and Mrs Clarke at the Fox and Goose are the inheritors of a quite remarkable tradition of hospitality in Fressingfield that goes back unbroken to the reign of Henry VIII. The inn was originally the Church House, or Guildhall, built for the explicit purpose of removing picnicking churchgoers from the nave of the church (they allowed such goings-on, it seems, in the sixteenth century) to more worldly premises. The church is still the landlord, and while Mrs Clarke is getting your meal you can gaze upon the graveyard or challenge Mr Clarke to a game of skittles (knock all nine down as he does, and there's a half-bottle of champagne on the house). Not that there'll be any delay, for you will have discussed and ordered your dinner before you arrived. This way Mrs Clarke can phone up Lowestoft in the morning for your fresh-caught sole or your fresh smoked eel, or Mr Clarke (an ex-butcher

himself) can have a word with Mr Spratt — truly! — about your piece of beef.

Kipper Pâté

2 8-oz packets of boil-in-the-bag kippers
2 oz of melted butter
The yolks of 2 hard-boiled eggs
¼ pint of double cream
Freshly milled black pepper

Boil the kippers according to the directions on the packet, then snip open the bag with some scissors, pour off the juices into a small bowl and keep on one side. Now remove the skins from the kippers, place the kippers in a largish bowl and mash well with a fork. Next add the yolks of the eggs, mash those in well, then add the double cream and kipper juices, and season with freshly milled black pepper. Pack the mixture into an earthenware dish and, when quite cold, pour over melted butter to cover. Chill, and serve with hot toast. (*Serves 8*)

Fillet of Beef Stroganoff

3 lb of beef fillet
6 tablespoons of meat stock
3 medium onions
1½ lb of button mushrooms
3 oz of butter
1½ tablespoons of oil
6 fl. oz of double cream
3 bay leaves
3 tablespoons of brandy
Salt, freshly milled black pepper

Cut the beef into even chunks or strips and season with salt and freshly milled black pepper. Peel and slice the onions, and if the mushrooms are large slice them in half. Heat the butter and oil, and fry the beef in it until it browns. Remove the beef from the pan and keep warm. In the same pan fry the onions and mushrooms till golden brown, then return the meat to the pan, and add the stock and bay leaves. Check the seasoning, cover the pan and let the meat simmer for ½ an hour on a low heat. Five minutes before serving add the cream and brandy. Serve on a large plate surrounded by rice. (*Serves 8*)

Raspberry Cream

2 lb of raspberries (fresh or frozen)
3 tablespoons of Orange Curaçao
½ lb of sugar
¾ pint of water
1 pint of double cream
A few lightly toasted almonds for decoration

Place the sugar and water in a saucepan and bring to the boil, without a lid on. Boil until the mixture is reduced by half, then allow it to cool. Meanwhile press the raspberries through a nylon sieve, then stir the cooled syrup and the Orange Curaçao into the raspberry pulp. Whip the double cream till thick and combine it very thoroughly with the raspberry mixture. Spoon the mixture into individual glasses, decorate with toasted almonds and chill before serving. (*Serves 8*)

The Oysterage

Orford, Suffolk
Orford 277

The Pinney empire at Orford is impressive by its very absence of glamour. The Oysterage, their famous restaurant in this Suffolk village, is self-admittedly more reminiscent of a caff – but tell us where else you could walk out with half a dozen oysters for 50p. Further on are their oyster-rearing farm and mussel beds fed by the clear, unpolluted waters of Butley Creek. This year, Mr Pinney said, they are beginning to hatch their own seed oysters, with the possibility of restoring the old Orford Native stock, and they are developing the new strain of all-the-year-round oysters known as Gigas. But it is for their smoke-houses that they are probably best-known. The Pinney method of smoking is unique, using whole oak logs in place of the conventional sawdust, and the houses have the capacity to run day and night. Festival-goers at nearby Aldeburgh will testify to the excellent results the Pinneys obtain, whether it's with trout, cod's roe, salmon or the local eels, and no doubt insist that such devotedly smoked fish need no fancy recipes to improve on them. Quite right, but the following recipes are genuine Pinney ones, and are for cooking at home, in the sad event that you can't get to Orford yourself.

Smoked Salmon and Cod's Roe Paste

6 oz of smoked cod's roe
6 oz of smoked salmon (off-cuts)
6 teaspoons of olive oil
6 teaspoons of lemon juice
1 clove of garlic (crushed)
Freshly grated nutmeg
Salt, freshly milled black pepper

First boil the cod's roe in water for about 10 minutes until it becomes granular in texture, drain and when cool remove the skin. Pass the smoked salmon through the fine disc of a mincer, then combine the cod's roe, crushed garlic and salmon together. Now whip in alternately a teaspoon of lemon juice then a teaspoon of oil, continuing to whip vigorously with a fork until all the lemon juice and oil is whipped in. Season with freshly milled black pepper and nutmeg, and a little salt if it needs it. Serve with thin slices of hot toast. (*Serves 6*)

Pork with Clams (or Cockles)

1 hand of pork
2 pigs' hocks (with trotters)

For the stock:
3 cloves of garlic
1 onion
1 small bunch of parsley
2 sprigs of thyme
2 bay leaves
Salt, freshly milled black pepper

The rest of the ingredients:
6 cloves of garlic (threaded onto one small thin skewer)
1 tablespoon of olive oil
2½ lb of potatoes (peeled and cut)
2 pints of clams in the shell (or cockles)
Beurre manié (made with 2 oz of butter and 2 oz of flour)
Salt and freshly milled black pepper

First cut all the meat off the 2 hocks and the hand of pork, and place the bones and trotters in a stockpot (discarding all the skin and fat etc). Put in the rest of the stock ingredients, fill up with water and simmer gently for 1½ hours.

All the trimmed meat should be cut into cubes slightly larger than 1 inch square, and placed in a baking tin (oiled with 1 tablespoon of olive oil). Season with salt and freshly milled black pepper, and tuck the skewered garlic down in the middle (threading the clams on a skewer or cocktail stick makes them easier to extract later). Place the tin in a pre-heated oven (300°F (mark 2)) and cook the pork slowly for 1½ hours, turning it once or twice during the cooking.

Meanwhile boil the potatoes till cooked but

still firm, and cut them in very thick slices. The clams or cockles should be placed in a thick saucepan or cooking pot on their own, and steamed with a lid on until open (about 10 minutes). Strain the clam liquor through some fine muslin and reserve it. Remove the clams from the shells. When the pork is cooked, pour off all the fat, extract the garlic, then pour in the clams and their liquor, and turn the oven up to 400°F (mark 6). Skim the fat from the stock, add 2 pints of stock to a saucepan and bring to simmering point, thickening with beurre manié added in pea-nut sized pieces. Cover the meat and clams with the potatoes, pour in the thickened stock and return the tin to the oven for 10 to 15 minutes. (Note: salted cockles can be used if well soaked first, but cockles in vinegar are unsuitable). (*Serves 8*)

The Pheasant

Keyston, Huntingdonshire
Bythorn 241

At Keyston, with its gabled cottages and well manicured gardens, you are literally in the very heart of England, and anything more English than this thatched and white-walled inn would be difficult to imagine. It has stood on the village green for nearly three and a half centuries and, although its attendant blacksmith's shop has disappeared, it looks as bright and hospitable as the day it was built. It is in fact the cornerstone of a small empire of inns in the area run by Mr Somerset Moore and his partners. Whether it's because he once worked at Prunier's, or perversely because whichever way you turn the coast is out of reach, he has built up an enviable reputation for shellfish at the Pheasant – even if it was an uphill struggle to reach a sale of a hundredweight of mussels a week. The adventurous menu is not, of course, confined to such things – indeed they'll cook anything that hunter, fisherman or gardener cares to bring along. It may interest you to know, if you're in a hurry to get to the Pheasant, that there's a landing strip at the back where you can bring in your private plane or helicopter if the wind's in the right direction (and hundreds do each year).

Clams with Garlic Butter

2 dozen clams (washed thoroughly in several changes of water)

For the garlic butter:
3 oz of breadcrumbs
3 tablespoons of fresh chopped parsley
1 or 2 cloves of garlic (crushed)
3 oz of butter
1 tablespoon of lemon juice
Salt, freshly milled black pepper
Some rock salt

First make the garlic butter by mixing all the ingredients thoroughly together with a fork. To open the clams you can either prise them open with a short-bladed knife (difficult) or, as Mr Somerset Moore suggests, simply drop them from the height of 2 feet flat-side down onto a hard floor (in which case you remove the pieces of splintered shell and wash thoroughly again). Cut the muscle that attaches the clam to the shell, then place the clams on a grill pan, on a bed of rock salt to prevent them tipping over. Now divide the butter and pile some on top of each clam. Pre-heat the grill, and grill them for 4 minutes, being very careful not to overcook or they will be tough. (*Serves 4*)

Quail Pie with Forcemeat

4 quail
2 oz of butter
Salt, freshly milled black pepper
½ lb of puff pastry
1 egg (beaten)

For the stuffing:
4 oz of sausage meat
1 level tablespoon of fresh chopped tarragon (or 1 level tablespoon if dried)
1 small onion (finely chopped)
Salt, freshly milled black pepper

For the sauce:
1½ oz of butter
1½ oz of flour
¾ pint of all-purpose stock (page 152)
¼ pint of red wine
¼ lb of mushrooms (sliced)
1 onion (chopped)
Fat for sautéing
Salt and freshly milled black pepper

Pre-heat the oven to 375°F (mark 5).

Make up the stuffing by mixing all the ingredients together thoroughly. Pre-cooking

it in the oven for 20 minutes, then stuff the birds with it. Season each one and rub the outsides generously with butter, roast them for 12 minutes at the above temperature, then remove them from the oven and turn the heat up to 425°F (mark 7).

To make the sauce, sauté the chopped onion and mushrooms for about 10 minutes, and while that's happening melt the butter in a small saucepan, stir in the flour till smooth, and gradually add the stock and the wine to make a smooth sauce. Taste and add seasoning then, using a draining spoon, add the onion and mushrooms. Place each quail in an individual pie dish, pour the sauce over and cover each one with a puff pastry lid. Make a few slits in the pastry, brush with beaten egg and bake in the oven for 15 to 20 minutes, or until the pastry has risen and turned golden brown. (*Serves 4*)

Greek Island Salad

6 oz of Fetta cheese (or failing that, White Stilton or Mozzarella)
6 large tomatoes (thinly sliced)
1 onion (finely chopped)
2 oz of black olives
2 oz of gherkins (sliced)
4 tablespoons of olive oil
Salt, freshly milled black pepper

Mix all the ingredients except the oil, with a seasoning of salt and freshly milled black pepper. Pour the olive oil evenly over the salad and leave it for a few minutes to percolate through. Either serve as a first course on its own, or as an accompaniment to a meat dish. (*Serves 4*)

The De La Poste

Swavesey, Cambridgeshire
Swavesey 241

The characteristically English fen country of windmills and water towers to the north of Cambridge is not the first place you'd look to find a truly genuine French country restaurant. But there it is, at the far end of Swavesey's pleasant village green, announcing itself discreetly with a plain weathered sign. Discretion is not the hallmark of the De La Poste, but perfection is. André Arama hails originally from Marseilles, and turns a deaf ear to his family's suggestions that perhaps he might return some day to France because, as he says, a French patron is so aloof from his clientèle and that isn't his style at all.

Mr Arama is devoted to your enjoyment of his food, and his anxiety takes him on regular trips to French ports to make sure of getting the fish he wants, and prompts him to discard a dish if he finds the smallest flaw in it (where most of us might not even recognise it as a flaw). After a memorable Sunday lunch with André Arama – who looks as classically French as his food tastes – even Swavesey began to take on a slight and beguiling Gallic air in the April sunshine, we promise.

Ficelés Picards

Delicately thin pancakes with ham and mushroom stuffing and a cream sauce.

For the pancakes:
2 oz of plain flour
2 whole eggs
1 tablespoon of oil
2 tablespoons of water
1 pinch of salt
¼ pint of milk
1 oz of melted butter
Butter for frying

For the filling and sauce:
1 small onion (chopped small)
1 oz of butter
1 tablespoon of chopped parsley
¼ lb of ham (chopped)
2 oz of mushrooms (chopped)
1 clove of garlic (crushed)
1 oz of breadcrumbs
1 level tablespoon of tomato purée
Freshly milled black pepper
¼ pint of double cream
3 oz of grated cheese
A little butter

First make the batter. Place the flour, salt, eggs, 1 tablespoon of oil and 2 tablespoons of water in a basin, and mix well and vigorously. Add sufficient milk (¼ pint) to make a thin batter. Add 1 oz of melted butter and

leave the batter to stand for an hour. Then make 6 large but very thin pancakes (in a pan about 10 inches in diameter).

In another frying pan fry the chopped onion in butter till softened, then add the parsley, ham and chopped mushrooms and cook for about 5 minutes. Then add the garlic and the tomato purée. Cook for a further 5 minutes, stir in the crumbs, season, then remove pan from the heat, mix well and the stuffing is ready. Put some of the stuffing into the centre of each pancake, fold over on all 4 sides, then fry the stuffed pancake in a little butter on each side, and arrange them in a flame-proof dish. Pour the cream into the frying pan, and bring it to the boil. Now pour it over the pancakes, sprinkle with grated cheese and brown lightly under a hot grill.

(Note: the pancakes can be made and stuffed in advance, then fried and coated with cream and cheese just before serving.) (*Serves 6*)

Boeuf à la Bourguignonne

2 lb shin of beef (cut into small squares)
2 oz of fat bacon (diced)
2 chopped onions
4 carrots (diced)
1 level teaspoon of dried thyme
1 bay leaf
1 clove of garlic (chopped)
1 level tablespoon of flour
¼ pint of beef stock (or water)
½ bottle of red Burgundy
1 unpeeled clove of garlic
1 tablespoon of fresh chopped parsley
Oil and butter
Salt, freshly milled black pepper

Pre-heat the oven to 325°F (mark 3).

Fry the meat in oil and butter to brown it nicely then transfer it to a flameproof casserole. In the same frying pan fry the diced bacon, chopped onions, carrots and parsley, a seasoning of salt and freshly milled black pepper, and a bay leaf – for about 10 minutes. Then transfer the vegetables etc to the casserole containing the beef. Place the casserole over the heat, and add 1 chopped clove of garlic, 1 tablespoon of flour and a little more salt and pepper. Stir and cook for 3 minutes, then gradually stir in the stock and red wine, and add a clove of unpeeled garlic. Stir well, bring to simmering point, cover and cook in the oven for about 2 hours or until the meat is tender.

For the garnish:
2 oz of lean bacon (diced)
½ lb of very small whole button onions
½ lb of small whole mushrooms
1½ oz of butter

Fry the onions in butter to brown all over for about 6 minutes, add the mushrooms and bacon, and cook for a few minutes more. Then add a ladleful of the sauce from the beef and cook for a further 3 minutes. Serve the beef with the garnish and steamed potatoes. (Note: the Boeuf à la Bourguignonne will taste better if allowed to cool and then reheated. Hence this meal can be made in the morning and served in the evening.) (*Serves 6*)

Parfait à la Vanille

6 egg yolks
4 oz of caster sugar
½ wineglass of water
1 coffeespoon of pure vanilla essence
1 liqueur glass of brandy
6 oz of double cream

Place the 6 egg yolks in a copper or stainless steel basin or saucepan (not aluminium). Boil 4 oz of sugar in ½ a wineglassful of water until the sugar has dissolved, then pour the mixture on to the egg yolks and whisk thoroughly. Now place the basin over a very low heat on the stove and cook slowly until the mixture coats the back of a spoon that you will dip in from time to time. Remove from the heat, stir in the vanilla essence and brandy, then allow the mixture to cool. Whisk the double cream until just beginning to thicken, then carefully mix it into the egg yolk mixture. Pour into individual dishes and freeze till firm in the ice-making compartment of the refrigerator – about 1 hour or so. (*Serves 6*)

The Pink Geranium

Melbourn, Cambridgeshire
Royston 60215

You do not see the best of Melbourn just driving through it on the way to Cambridge. You may catch a glimpse of the twelfth-century church, but you would almost certainly miss the Pink Geranium, just off to the left. Once it was a tea shop – hence the inherited name – now it is Mrs Shepperson's highly-rated restaurant. If the name is evocative, then so are the surroundings: the early seventeenth-century thatched cottage (once three dwellings with a communal pump and chimney for cooking, which is still a focal point of the dining room) is surrounded by a riot of flowers in summer and glows with candlelight in winter. The menu, like the place, is compact, allowing the same attention to detail which is evident throughout the restaurant. In addition to being a successful chef, Gerry Stewart also somehow finds time to be a successful writer, now working on his third novel.

Pâté Maison

1 lb of fat pork (belly)
1 lb of lean veal
½ lb of pig's liver
4 fl. oz of dry white wine
1 fat clove of garlic (crushed)
6 peppercorns (crushed)
¼ lb of fat bacon (cut into small dice)
1 tablespoon of brandy
A little salt

Pre-heat the oven to 300°F (mark 2).

Mince the pork, veal and liver (or have the butcher do this for you) and combine the three together with the chopped bacon. Add the garlic, crushed peppercorns, wine, brandy and salt and mix thoroughly. Pack the mixture into a 2-pint terrine, place the terrine in a roasting tin half-filled with water and bake slowly for 1½ hours or until the pâté starts to come away from the sides of the terrine. Remove from the oven, leave to cool, and if you need to store it for any length of time, pour melted lard over the surface to seal. Before serving, pass the pâté (without the lard) through the mincer again. Serve in individual portions on lettuce. (*Serves 10*)

Duck with Cointreau Sauce

1 fresh duck (5 to 6 lb)
4 teaspoons of Cointreau
Salt, freshly milled black pepper

For the sauce:
1½ oz of butter
1½ level tablespoons of flour
½ pint of milk
The grated rind and juice of 1 orange
The grated rind and juice of ½ lemon
1 level tablespoon of caster sugar
1½ tablespoons of Cointreau
2 tablespoons of double cream

Pre-heat the oven to 450°F (mark 8).

Season the duck with salt and freshly milled black pepper, wrap it securely in foil in a baking tin, and cook for 3 hours in a very hot oven. During the last 20 minutes or so, pull back the foil, pour off the excess fat, return the duck to the oven and allow it to crisp on the outside. While the duck is cooking, pre-pare the sauce by melting the butter in a thick saucepan, stirring in the flour, then adding the milk bit by bit (still stirring) to make a smooth white sauce. Season, then allow the sauce to cook very, very gently for 10 minutes, then stir in the orange and lemon juice and grated rinds, followed by the sugar, the Cointreau and finally the cream. Carve the duck into 4 portions, pour a teaspoon of Cointreau over each portion, and serve the sauce separately. (*Serves 4*)

Tipsy Cake

1 7-inch round Genoese sponge (see Baked Alaska, page 117)
1 dessert apple (chopped with the peel left on)
1 orange (peeled, pith removed, and chopped)
1 pear (peeled and sliced)
1 banana (peeled and sliced)
1 tablespoon of lemon juice
4 oz of grapes (peeled, halved and pipped)
4 tablespoons of sweet sherry
½ pint of whipped cream
1 level tablespoon of caster sugar

Sprinkle the sponge base (placed on a serving dish) with 3 tablespoons of sweet Spanish sherry and leave it to soak for a couple of hours. Prepare the fruit by sprinkling with sugar and lemon juice, and chilling till needed. Just before serving, strain the fruit to remove the juice, pile onto the cake, sprinkle with the remaining tablespoon of sherry, and top with whipped cream. Serve cut into wedges. (*Serves 4*)

Swan House

Fowlmere, Cambridgeshire
Fowlmere 444

The Swan House is the youngest of all the establishments we visited on our travels – at the time it had been a restaurant for barely a year, though its reincarnation followed a pattern already familiar elsewhere. Like many other places it had originally been an inn (the Swan) in the early eighteenth century before it settled into a private existence as a farm, and the magnificent chimney in the dining room (which now houses the opulent cold table) testifies to some lusty cooking in Georgian days.

The cooking here now is the work of a young Frenchman, Jean-Louis Maurin, who learned his profession in a restaurant in Alsace and learned it quite superbly. As he took us layer by layer through his Hot Mousseline of Sole, the imagination leapt; but the real thing when it arrived was even more beautiful than it sounded. Rumours of such food, naturally, do not take long to reach Cambridge, only eight miles away, and the Swan House is already popular with dons seeking to escape for a while from the rigours of the High Table.

Hot Mousseline of Sole

For stage one:
1 lb of fresh fillets of sole
¼ pint of double cream
2 large egg whites
Salt, cayenne pepper
The juice of ¼ lemon (approx 1 dessert-
    spoon)
1 teaspoon of brandy

For stage two:
8 oz of freshly-made white breadcrumbs
4 dessertspoons of chopped parsley
1 dessertspoon of snipped chives
1 dessertspoon of fresh chopped tarragon
1 egg (separated)
1 whole egg
6 fresh asparagus stalks, medium size
    (trimmed and washed)
A few green fennel tops (if available)
½ lb of back pork fat (cut into very thin slices
    —lardons)

Stage one: keep 4 whole fillets aside and put the rest through the fine blade of the mincer. Season the minced sole with salt and a little cayenne pepper, then place it in a bowl fitted over another bowl full of ice cubes and leave it like that for 2 hours. Then whisk the egg whites till stiff, fold them into the fish, and then fold in half the cream (which should be lightly whipped first until it's just beginning to thicken).

Stage two: in a basin mix the breadcrumbs with the herbs, add 1 egg yolk and 1 complete egg, mix thoroughly, and finally mix in the rest of the cream and a light seasoning of salt and cayenne pepper. Now prepare a heavy oblong terrine about 9″ × 3″ (Le Creuset

make one of this size) by lining it with wafer-thin slices of pork fat, pressing them well all round. Lay a few fennel tops along the centre of the base. Whisk the remaining egg white, then put half of the *stage one* mixture into the terrine, season 2 of the whole fillets, dip them in the egg white and lay on top of the mixture. Then put half of the *stage two* mixture in, and on top of that lay 6 asparagus stalks. Now add the other half of the *stage two* mixture, followed by the other two whole fillets (again seasoned and dipped in beaten egg white first) and finally the last layer – the rest of the *stage one* mixture. Cover the mousseline with more thin slices of pork fat and put on the lid.

Place the terrine in a roasting tin half-filled with warm water and bake in a pre-heated oven 325°F (mark 3) for 1¼ hours. Loosen the edges and turn the pâté out onto an oblong serving dish. Cut in slices and serve with Hollandaise sauce (see page 151). It can also be eaten cold.

Note: this recipe sounds a lot more complicated than it is, but after you've made it the first time it really does become quite easy. (*Serves 12*)

Paupiettes de Veau with Cucumbers

6 veal escalopes (beaten out flat)
6 rashers of smoked streaky bacon (rinded)
½ large cucumber
¼ pint of double cream
5 fl. oz of dry white wine
2 level tablespoons of seasoned flour
2 to 3 oz of butter
Salt, freshly milled black pepper

For the stuffing:
8 oz of minced pork
5 oz of fresh white breadcrumbs
1 egg
1 dessertspoon of fresh chopped parsley
Salt, freshly milled black pepper
A pinch of paprika

For the garnish:
¼ lb of mushrooms
¼ lb of button onions (peeled)
Oil and butter

Pre-heat the oven to 400°F (mark 6).

Mix all the stuffing ingredients together, seasoning well. Lay a piece of bacon on each escalope, season, then put some of the stuffing on the centre of each one; roll them up neatly and tie with string. Now dust each one with seasoned flour and fry in butter to a golden brown on all sides. Transfer the paupiettes to a wide casserole, cover and cook them in the oven for 20 minutes.

Prepare the cucumber by peeling it, splitting it in half lengthways and scooping out the seeds. Then chop the cucumber into small dice, pour cold water over them to blanch,

111

and drain well. When the 20 minutes are up add the cucumber to the casserole plus the wine and cream, stirring round a bit, put the lid back on and return the casserole to the oven for a further 10 minutes. Meanwhile brown the onions and mushrooms in oil and butter for the garnish. To serve, place the paupiettes on a warm serving dish, with all the sauce poured over and a garnish of mushrooms and button onions. (*Serves* 6)

Soufflé Grand Marnier

8 large eggs (use all the whites and 6 yolks)
1 pint of milk
6 oz of caster sugar
2 oz of butter
2 oz of cornflour
3 fl. oz of Grand Marnier

Pre-heat the oven to 350°F (mark 4).

In a thick saucepan add the sugar to the milk and bring to the boil. In a second saucepan, melt the butter and add the corn-flour. Mix well, then gradually pour in the milk, stirring continuously until smooth and creamy. Turn out into a mixing-bowl and allow to cool for 2 minutes. Pour in the Grand Marnier and the 6 egg yolks and beat well.
The egg whites should be beaten till stiff and carefully folded into the mixture, then the whole lot poured into a buttered 3-pint soufflé dish and baked in the oven for 20 minutes. (*Serves* 6)

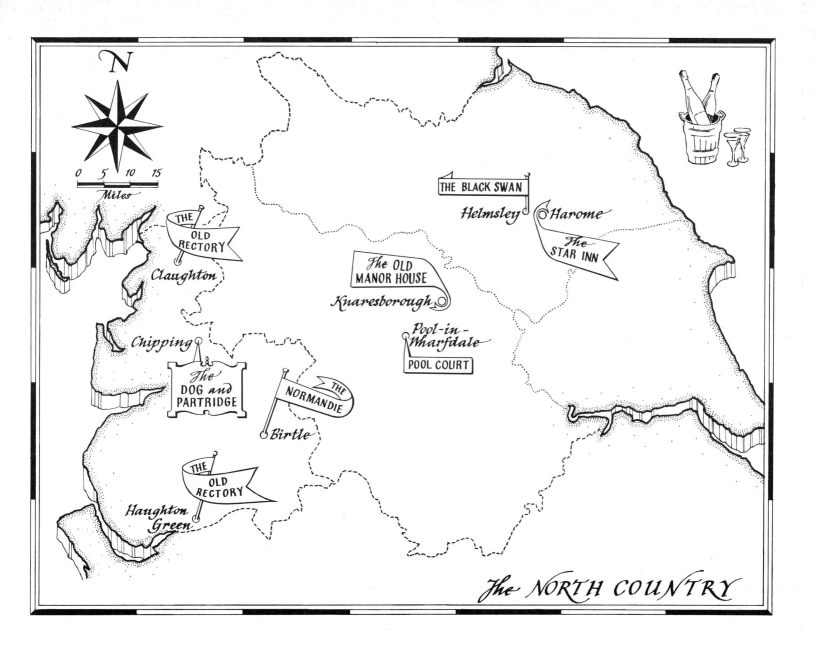

N

0 5 10 15
Miles

THE OLD RECTORY
Claughton

THE BLACK SWAN
Helmsley   Harome
The STAR INN

The OLD MANOR HOUSE
Knaresborough

Pool-in-Wharfdale
POOL COURT

Chipping

The DOG and PARTRIDGE

THE NORMANDIE
Birtle

THE OLD RECTORY
Haughton Green

The NORTH COUNTRY

The Old Rectory

Claughton, Lancashire
Hornby 455

The lovely Lune Valley, across which the village of Claughton looks, is famous for its salmon. Morecombe Bay just down the road is famous for its shrimps (that is, when the whitebait don't occasionally take over). The twelfth-century Claughton church is famous for having the oldest cast bell in the British Isles. The Old Rectory long ago severed its ecclesiastical connections in favour of culinary ones – though the aged bell is still at hand and apt to give a periodic clonk to remind you of what the house once was.

Mrs Martin, with her heart and her cooking firmly rooted in Lancashire, has offered an individual and distinguished

table at the old Georgian rectory for seven years past. She can't remember when the neighbouring manor house was shifted brick by brick up to the top of the hill by descendents of Samuel Morse, the inventor of morse code, but she does recall the days when – before a disastrous flood – a trout stream conveniently flowed through the garden. (Trout still figures strongly on the menu, and perhaps it's some consolation that a new smokehouse in nearby Lancaster is gaining a high local reputation.)

Peanut Soup

½ **small chicken**
1 **large onion**
4 **oz of salted peanuts**
1 **oz of unsalted butter**
½ **pint of gold top milk**
¼ **pint of double cream**
1 **small glass of sherry**
Salt, pepper, whole black peppercorns

Cut the chicken into 3 or 4 pieces, removing the fat, and place the pieces in a saucepan together with half the onion, sliced. Add salt, half a dozen peppercorns and approximately 2½ pints of water and simmer gently over a gentle heat to make a strong stock (this will take about 2½ to 3 hours).
To make the soup, gently sauté the other half of the onion in butter to soften. Rub the peanuts in a cloth to get rid of the salt, then pulverise them in a grinder or liquidiser. When the onions are soft, add the nuts and stir them around for 5 to 10 minutes. Strain the stock, skim off any fat, measure 2 pints and add it to the nuts and onions – then simmer gently for ½ an hour. Taste, add salt and pepper if necessary, then stir in the sherry and milk and bring to the boil. Turn the heat off, put a lid on the pan and leave overnight. The following day – just before you're ready to serve the soup – add the cream. Heat through without boiling and serve immediately. (*Serves 6*)

Mrs Martin's Lancashire Hotpot

3 **lb of neck of mutton (middle and best end)**
1 **lb of stewing beef**
2 **sheep's kidneys**
3 **lb of potatoes (cut into thickish slices)**
1 **lb of carrots (sliced)**
1 **large onion**
¾ **pint of good stock (or a cube)**
Seasoned flour, dripping
Salt, freshly milled black pepper
A little butter

Pre-heat the oven to 325°F (mark 3).

Cut the beef into bite-size pieces and roll both the beef and the mutton in seasoned flour, then fry all the meat in dripping to brown and seal on both sides. Do this bit by bit, so as not to overcrowd the pan. Keep the browned meat on one side while you fry the onion to soften it a little. Take a suitably sized casserole (Mrs Martin recommends a good old brown stewpot), arrange a layer of sliced potatoes over the bottom, fill up with the meat, carrots, onion and potatoes, seasoning with freshly milled black pepper and salt as you go, and finishing with a layer of potatoes on the top overlapping each other. Lift one corner of the potatoes, pour in the stock, then melt some butter and brush it over the top of the potatoes. Now put a lid on the casserole and cook for 2 hours in the oven, removing the lid during the last ½ hour to brown the top. (This dish goes very well with spiced red cabbage – my suggestion DS.) (*Serves 6*)

Lancaster Lemon Tart

3 **rounded tablespoons of lemon curd**
3 **oz of butter or margarine (room temperature)**
3 **oz of caster sugar**
1 **egg (beaten lightly)**
1 **oz of ground almonds**
The grated rind and juice of 1 lemon
1½ **oz of whole almonds (peeled and halved)**
4 **oz of self-raising flour**
4 **oz of shortcrust pastry**

Pre-heat the oven to 400°F (mark 6).

Line a 7- or 8-inch pie plate with pastry and spread the base with lemon curd. Now cream the butter and sugar together till light, pale and fluffy, and beat in the beaten egg, bit by bit. Next fold in the ground almonds and flour, followed by the lemon rind and juice. Spread the mixture over the lemon curd and smooth with a palette knife. Sprinkle the halved almonds on the surface, bake in the centre of the oven for 15 minutes then reduce the heat to 300°F (mark 2) and continue cooking for a further 25 to 30 minutes. Serve either warm or cold, with cream. (*Serves 6*)

The Dog and Partridge

Chipping, Lancashire
Chipping 201

Records show this Tetley's inn goes back at least as far as 1515, and the thickness of its walls suggest even further. It was called the Cliviger Arms then, after the local gentry, and in 1715 changed its name to the Green Man for the next hundred and fifty years, during which period it was used as the setting for a popular play called *The Raven* (whose plot appears to have involved a Methodist minister, an Anglican priest and two of the inn rooms, still called the Pink and Green rooms). How a small inn deep in the Lancashire fells took to the stage at all must remain a mystery, but its present reputation – if less dramatic – is based on something rather more substantial. And that is Mrs Barr's cooking. As her husband says, it is honest and unadorned, but if ever proof was needed that a respect for flavour, the very freshest of materials and a bottomless stockpot can turn a simple meal into a great one, it is to be found at the Dog and Partridge.

Duck Soup

For the stock:
1 duck carcass (broken up)
Duck giblets
1 onion (stuck with 2 cloves)
2 medium carrots (roughly chopped)
1 leek (cleaned and sliced)
1 stick of celery (roughly chopped) and a few
　celery tops
1 bay leaf
1 small bunch of parsley
Salt

For the soup:
Stock as above
2 oz of butter
1 tablespoon of flour
2 carrots (thinly sliced)
1 onion (chopped small)
1 stick of celery (chopped small)
A little grated orange rind
1 tablespoon of fresh chopped parsley
Salt, freshly milled black pepper

To make the stock, place all the ingredients in a large saucepan with enough water to cover (approx 2½ pints). Bring slowly to simmering point, take off any scum from the surface, cover and simmer very, very gently for 3 or 4 hours. Then strain the stock through a fine sieve and discard all the débris. To make the soup, melt the butter in a large thick saucepan, add the chopped vegetables, stir them round and let them sweat for 10 minutes with the lid on and the heat very low. Now sprinkle in the flour, stir and add the stock bit by bit. Bring to simmering point and simmer (without a lid) until the vegetables are tender – about 15 minutes. Taste to check the seasoning, add a little grated orange rind and sprinkle the parsley over before serving. (*Serves 4 or 6*)

Baked Alaska Flambé

For the sponge:
2 oz of plain flour
2 oz of caster sugar
2 eggs

The rest of the ingredients:
1 family block of vanilla and strawberry ice
　cream
4 pineapple rings
3 large egg whites
6 oz of caster sugar
3 tablespoons of brandy
1 tablespoon of Grand Marnier

Pre-heat the oven to 375°F (mark 5).

Take a 7-inch sandwich tin approx. 1½ inches deep, grease well and dust lightly with flour and caster sugar.

First make the sponge. Put the eggs and sugar in a mixing bowl and whisk with an electric mixer until the mixture is pale and creamy, and thick enough to leave a trail when the mixer is lifted out for a few seconds. Now, using a metal spoon, carefully fold in half the flour first, and then the other half. Pour the mixture into the prepared tin and bake near the top of the oven for 20 to 25 minutes or until well risen and firm to touch in the centre. Allow to cool for a few minutes in the tin, then turn out onto a wire cooling rack.

The baked Alaska should be prepared just before serving. Pre-heat the oven to 450°F (mark 8). Place the sponge on a heat-proof serving dish and sprinkle it with 1 tablespoon of brandy. Beat the egg whites till stiff, then gradually beat in the sugar a little at a time to a stiff meringue. Place the ice cream block on the sponge, arrange the pineapple on top, then spoon the meringue over taking it all round the edge of the dish to seal the ice cream in completely. Place the dish in the oven and cook for 3 or 4 minutes, or until the meringue begins to brown. Heat the remaining brandy with the Grand Marnier in a ladle, set light to it and pour it flaming over the baked Alaska at the table. Serve at once. (*Serves 4*)

The Normandie

Birtle, Lancashire
061-764 3869

Some years ago a Champeau married a Jenkinson and now there is a little bit of France up in the hills above Bury. Marriage – and the gastronomic poverty of the Manchester area fifteen years ago – are what brought Mr Champeau to this spot rather than the fact (which he puts about) that there was no room in France for him and de Gaulle – though it's said thereabouts that he can be imperious, too, especially with latecomers. But we found him in jovial mood, not to say romantic. The night-time view from the Normandie, when the distant chimney stacks driven into the guts of the landscape like nails are invisible, was 'just like the harbour at Cannes', he insisted.

The drive up twisting country lanes to this converted farmhouse is seemingly endless, but the peak when you achieve it is a culinary one rather than geographic. Mr Champeau's brother has now joined him and they both cook the French, especially Normandy, specialities for which the restaurant is justly famous. That goes for the wines as well, which have been built up round their father-in-law's discovery of the Cellar of a deceased water engineer, and now even include a few 'mise en bouteille à Birtle'.

'Normandie' Soupe de Poisson

1 lb of fillet of sole (cut into small strips)
½ lb of prawns (peeled)
½ lb of scampi
Salt, freshly milled black pepper
1 sachet of powdered saffron (1·9 grams)
2 medium onions (sliced)
2 medium carrots (sliced)
2 leeks, white parts only (sliced)
2 level tablespoons of butter
1½ pints of good fish stock (see page 152)
Olive oil
Seasoned flour

Heat the butter in a large saucepan and sauté the sliced vegetables gently without browning. Keeping the heat low, cover and allow the vegetables to sweat for about 10 to 15 minutes. Strain the fish stock over the vegetables, sprinkle in the saffron, cover and simmer gently for 20 minutes. Meanwhile toss the sole and shellfish in seasoned flour and fry them in hot olive oil till golden (you'll probably have to do this in about 3 or 4 batches, depending on how large your frying pan is). Drain the fish pieces on crumpled paper, then add them to the soup. Season to taste with salt and freshly milled black pepper, bring to simmering point again, and simmer for 5 minutes. (*Serves 4 or 6*)

Canard Bon Homme Normand

1 fresh duckling (weighing 6 lb)
Salt, freshly milled black pepper
2 9½ oz bottles of cider
1 pint of double cream
2 level tablespoons of butter
2 fl. oz of Calvados
4 tart dessert apples (peeled and cut into dice)

Pre-heat the oven to 400°F (mark 6).

Rub the duck inside and out with salt and freshly milled black pepper. Wrap it loosely but securely in see-through cooking wrap, place it in a roasting tin and three-quarters cook it for 1½ hours. Meanwhile pour the cider into a saucepan and boil briskly until it has reduced down to a dark syrupy mixture making about 2 tablespoons, then remove it from the heat and keep on one side.

When the duck has been cooking for 1½ hours, remove it from the foil, pour off the fat from the juices and to the juices left in the roasting tin add the cream. Stir over a low heat to amalgamate. When it comes to the boil, pour this mixture into the saucepan containing the reduced cider.

The duck should be carved by removing the wing and leg joints and cutting the breast into long thin strips. Wrap the breast pieces in foil and keep warm; place the legs and wings in a warmed casserole. Pour the cream sauce over the legs and wings, cover and cook in the oven for a further 15 minutes.

Meanwhile melt the butter in a saucepan, add the Calvados and then the apples. Put a lid on, turn the heat up and cook the apples very quickly, shaking the pan all the time to prevent them sticking. They should be just cooked in about 6 to 8 minutes – but on no account must they be overcooked or mushy. When the apples are ready, arrange the slices of breast over the legs, wings, etc, pour the apples all over, and serve immediately with boiled potatoes and chilled cider. (*Serves 4*)

119

The Old Rectory

Haughton Green, Denton, Lancashire
(061 336) 7516

If it weren't for the fertile oasis of the Old Rectory, Haughton Green would certainly belie its name, for it has long been caught up and overtaken by red sprawl. However, down by the side of the church (modelled, you'd swear, on a Swiss chalet) a leafy lane takes you into the heart of the Old Rectory grounds, and here in summer by the fountain and fishpool you could indeed cherish the illusion of having got away from it all.

For some years under Mr Challenor-Chadwick the Old Rectory was a private dining club – perhaps a reaction against his previous crowded, beer-drinking pub in Derbyshire. But last year he was persuaded of the cruel unfairness of confining his superb food to businessmen, and threw open his door to the public once again. Mr Chadwick is a born host and raconteur, a devastating critic of fussy food or pompous service and an ardent champion of freshness and seasonal foods. His cooking speaks as eloquently.

Snails Old Rectory

2 dozen tinned snails
2 dozen small mushroom caps
6 to 8 oz of butter
2 cloves of garlic (crushed)
2 heaped tablespoons of fresh chopped parsley
1 teaspoon of lemon juice (approx)
Salt, freshly milled black pepper

First lightly cook the mushroom caps in butter with a squeeze of lemon juice, and keep warm. Rinse the snails. Melt 6 oz of butter in a saucepan, add the garlic and parsley, with some seasoning and finally the snails to warm through. Place one snail on each upturned mushroom cap, pour the butter over and serve at once, accompanied by brown bread and butter. (*Serves 4*)

Fegato alla Veneziana

1 lb of lamb's liver (Mr Chadwick suggests that you ask your butcher to skin and freeze the liver overnight and then slice it paper thin on his bacon-slicer. Alternatively you could freeze it in your own freezing compartment and slice it as thin as you can with a very sharp knife)
½ pint of red wine
2 medium onions (finely sliced)
1 level dessertspoon of powdered oregano
1 level tablespoon of flour
Salt, freshly milled black pepper
A little butter

Arrange the thin slices of liver in a shallow dish sprinkled with powdered oregano. Pour the wine over and leave it to marinade for at least 8 hours or overnight.

Cook the finely sliced onions in butter till soft (about 10 to 15 minutes), sprinkle in the flour, then stir in the marinade gradually to make a sauce – and add a bit more wine if you think it needs it. The liver slices should be stiffened and turned very quickly in hot butter – but be careful not to overcook. Serve the liver with the onion wine sauce poured over. (*Serves 4*)

Zabaglione

8 egg yolks
8 level dessertspoons of caster sugar
8 small sherry glasses of Marsala

Combine these ingredients either in a liquidiser or by beating till frothy. Pour the mixture into a double saucepan, and cook stirring gently till it has thickened. Serve immediately in warmed stemmed glasses. (*Serves 4*)

121

The Black Swan

Helmsley, Yorkshire
Helmsley 466

There are any number of reasons for coming to Helmsley, a civilised outpost of the Yorkshire moors. You might wish to inspect this pretty market town itself, or Rievaulx Abbey just two miles away, whose ruined magnificence inspired Turner. Or, come the Glorious Twelfth, you might assemble your guns here and sally forth to do battle with the grouse on the moors. Or you may just want to get away from it all at the Black Swan, which occupies a generous portion of one side of the market square. Part Tudor (the end that seems to be trespassing on the church-yard) and part Georgian, in its time it has been pub, farm, vicarage and hospital. Today as a hotel it is distinguished by its cooking as well as its comfort, and strangers to the North Riding like us appreciate that Mr and Mrs Hopper make a point of offering a wide variety of Yorkshire specialities, just as the pheasant-shooters appreciate their hot punch when the wind bites across the riggs.

122

Chicken Dales Style

4 chicken breasts (skin and bones removed)
4 oz of Wensleydale cheese (crumbled)
1 egg (beaten)
Seasoned flour
4 heaped tablespoons of fine white bread-
    crumbs
1 bunch of watercress
Oil (for frying)

For the sauce:
1 pint of milk
1 tablespoon of chopped fennel (or if out of
    season, ¼ level teaspoon of dried fennel
    seeds)
1 oz of butter
1 oz of flour
2 oz of chopped ham
Salt, freshly milled black pepper

Place the milk in a saucepan together with the fennel and some salt and pepper, put it on a very low heat to infuse (without coming to the boil) for 10 to 15 minutes. Strain the liquid and use it to make a white sauce with the butter and flour. Cook the sauce over a gentle heat for about 5 to 6 minutes, then add the ham. Check the seasoning and keep warm.

To prepare the chicken, cut a pocket on the inside of each breast, using a sharp knife, and fill the pocket with the crumbled cheese. Now dust each chicken portion in seasoned flour, then dip in beaten egg and roll in breadcrumbs, pressing them evenly all round. Deep fry the chicken in medium hot oil for about 10 minutes or until golden brown. Drain well on kitchen paper, and serve with fresh watercress, and the sauce handed round separately.

Yorkshire Curd Tart

½ lb of curds
3 level tablespoons of sugar
1 egg
A walnut of butter
2 oz of currants
A little chopped candied peel
A little nutmeg
1 level teaspoon of baking powder
4 oz of shortcrust pastry

Pre-heat the oven to gas mark 6 (400°F)

Break up the curds with a fork and add the currants and peel, sugar, baking powder and nutmeg. Now add the egg (well whisked) and, lastly, the butter (melted). Line a 7- or 8-inch tart tin with shortcrust pastry and put in the filling. Place on a baking sheet in the oven and bake until golden brown (about 30 minutes). Note: 1 tablespoon of golden syrup used in place of some of the sugar will give a shiny finish. (*Serves 4 to 6*)

123

The Old Manor House

Knaresborough, Yorkshire
Knaresborough 3332

Knaresborough must have seen a few royal feasts in its day, when it was the sporting centre for the mediaeval Kings of England. Indeed the Old Manor House served King John as his hunting lodge on more than one occasion, and several of the Yorkist monarchs are known to have wined and dined here. Almost everything about the house betrays its antiquity — although the fine panelling in the dining room is comparatively young (seventeenth century). One of the panels in the entrance hall even opens up, to reveal a tree, no less, around which the whole edifice has been constructed! The building is, rightly, an historical monument, but even without its royal associations its position alone would justify preservation. It stands amid a cluster of ancient houses which tumble down to the edge of the River Nidd (which deserves a much more beautiful name) as it slices through the town and under its imposing viaduct.

Mr Schwaller now presides over the Old Manor House with due respect for its history: his game soup is a rare piece of kitchen alchemy. Yet, even as it bubbled away on the stove, we tasted his Gâteau Grison and *knew* what we would ask him for.

Solothurner Platte

1 lb of fillet steak (in one piece)
2 medium onions (chopped)
¼ lb of dark-gilled mushrooms (sliced)
1 small green or red pepper (chopped)
¼ lb of Emmenthal cheese (cut into paper-thin slices)
¼ pint of Espagnole sauce (see page 152)
6 tablespoons of Madeira
4 tablespoons of cream
Salt, freshly milled black pepper
Butter

Pre-heat oven to very low (250°F (mark ½))

Using your sharpest knife, cut the fillet into 12 thin slices (3 per person) and season them with salt and freshly milled black pepper. Then in a very large frying pan melt some butter and lightly fry the onions, mushrooms and peppers for about 10 to 15 minutes, or until soft. Using a slotted spoon transfer the vegetable mixture on to a warm serving dish and keep warm in the oven. Add a little more butter to the pan, then fry the slices of fillet and brown them on both sides. When brown add the Madeira, let it bubble a bit, then remove the fillets and arrange on top of the pepper and onion mixture, placing a slice of Emmenthal cheese between the fillets. Keep it warm in the oven. To the juices left in the pan add the Espagnole sauce, bring to simmering point, then stir in the cream. Pour the sauce over the meat, and serve immediately. (*Serves 4*)

Gâteau Grison

For the pastry:
6 oz of plain flour
3 oz of butter
1 standard egg
2 level tablespoons of caster sugar

For the filling:
½ lb of soft brown sugar
4 tablespoons of water
½ lb of walnuts (roughly chopped)
¾ pint of double cream
2 tablespoons of very finely chopped hazel-nuts

To make the pastry case, break the egg into a basin, beat in the sugar; then sift the flour into a bowl and rub in the butter till the mixture resembles fine breadcrumbs. Now add the sugar and egg mixture to make a stiff paste. Roll out the pastry on a lightly floured board, and line a greased 8-inch flan tin. Now prick the base of the pastry with a fork and put it into the refrigerator for 30 minutes. Meanwhile pre-heat the oven to 400°F (mark 6). Line the pastry case with foil, fill with baking beans or rice, place on a baking sheet in the oven and cook for 20 minutes. Then remove the foil and beans, reduce the heat to 375°F (mark 5) and continue cooking for a further 10 minutes until the case is crisp and golden.

While the pastry case is cooking, prepare the filling by placing the sugar and water in a solid, light-coloured saucepan and bring the mixture very slowly to the boil, stirring now and then – it should be on a very low heat and will take about 10 minutes to come to the boil. When the sugar has completely dissolved, turn the heat up and boil for about 2 or 3 minutes until the mixture becomes dark and syrupy – don't overdo this though, or you'll have hard toffee on your hands. Remove the pan from the heat, stir in the walnuts, return the pan to the heat, bring to simmering point again. Then remove from the heat and pour in ¼ pint of the cream. Finally bring to the boil once more, then pour into the pastry case and leave in a cool place to set. Before serving, whip the remaining ½ pint of cream, spread it over the flan and sprinkle with finely chopped hazel-nuts. (*Serves 6 or 8*)

Pool Court

Pool-in-Wharfedale, Yorkshire
Arthington 2288

After the river Wharf has left the rugged-ness of the Yorkshire moors it enters into the gentler woolman's country. In Georgian times Pool Court was a wool merchant's house, and it testifies to the elegant living which such trade brought. The mills are closing now, but the house has retained its style – as a restaurant opened quite recently by Michael Gill. He hadn't yet, he told us, achieved everything he set out to do, but what he

has achieved, along with chef David Armstrong, seemed to us impressive enough. Television viewers in the region probably know of Mr Armstrong's touch, and his reputation extends far beyond, of course. But a closer acquaintance, with a chance of actually sampling his work, would be more than worth the effort, you may be assured.

Stilton Croquettes

4 oz of butter
4 oz of flour
½ pint of milk
4 oz of Stilton (mashed with a fork)
2 oz of celery
2 egg yolks
2 whole eggs (beaten)
Seasoned flour
Fresh white breadcrumbs
Oil for deep frying
Fresh tomato sauce (see page 151)

Start by chopping the celery finely and cooking it gently in very little water to soften. Then drain well and keep on one side. Now make a heavy thick béchamel base, using 4 oz of butter, 4 oz of flour and ½ pint of milk. Cook for a minute or two, stirring continuously, then beat in the egg yolks, the mashed Stilton, and finally the celery. Spread out the mixture on a plate or tray and allow it to 'set' in the refrigerator for 30 minutes or so. When the mixture is firm enough, roll it into walnut-sized balls, coat them first with flour, then with beaten egg. Roll them in breadcrumbs and deep fry till golden. Serve with fresh tomato sauce. (*Serves 6*)

Petit Homard Pool Court

Ideally fresh lobster tails should be used, but Dublin Bay prawns or scampi make excellent alternatives.

1 lb of fresh baby lobster tails
3 small shallots (finely chopped)
1 clove of garlic (crushed)
¼ lb of button mushrooms (finely sliced)
2 to 3 oz of butter
¼ pint of dry white Vermouth
¼ pint of double cream
1 egg yolk
Seasoned flour
Salt, freshly milled black pepper

Split the lobster tails and toss them lightly in seasoned flour, then fry them quickly in butter just to seal. Add the mushrooms, garlic and shallots to the pan as well, and cook everything together for about 3 minutes. Now, using a draining spoon, transfer everything to a serving dish and keep warm. Pour off most of the butter, then add the Vermouth to the pan and let it bubble and reduce by about a half. Have ready the egg yolk beaten into the cream, stir it into the Vermouth (off the heat), taste to check the seasoning, pour the sauce over the lobster, and serve at once with savoury rice. (*Serves 4*)

Amaretti Schokoladentorte

A 1½ lb box of Amaretti biscuits (from a delicatessen)
4 tablespoons of brandy
3 tablespoons of cider
6 oz of plain dessert chocolate
¾ pint of double cream
Whipped cream and
Grated chocolate, for decoration

Break up the chocolate into a basin fitted over a pan of barely simmering water and leave until melted. Meanwhile pour the cream into a saucepan and heat to just below boiling point. Pour the hot cream onto the melted chocolate and whisk (preferably with an electric mixer) until the mixture is a cold rich chocolate cream. Mix the brandy and the cider together. Now dip the biscuits a few at a time into the brandy and cider, then into the chocolate cream and arrange about 4 to 5 in the base of a 2¾-pint pudding basin. Next spread a layer of the chocolate mixture over the first layer of biscuits, then repeat the whole process until 4 layers are reached. Place a saucer (one that fits inside the rim) on top of the mixture, place a 2 or 3 lb weight on the saucer and leave in the refrigerator overnight. Before serving dip the basin in hot water for about 3 seconds, turn the pudding out onto a serving dish, allow the outside to get firm again, then decorate with whipped cream and grated chocolate. Serve cut into slices. (*Serves 6*)

127

The Star Inn

Harome, Yorkshire
Helmsley 397

Not without good reason was this inn in 1972 nominated Britain's Pub of the Year. It is everything you look for in an English country inn. It has stood on the edge of the North Yorkshire moors for six hundred years and still serves Old Peculiar to its local domino-playing customers, modestly for all its new-found fame. It is rich in rustic treasures; a formidable bench-seat in the dining room reveals, on close inspection, the inscriptions of four Cromwellian generals. The furniture in the bar and indeed the bar itself is original 'Mouseman' – a renowned local craftsman whose trademark was a mouse. Somewhere every stick of furniture carries one of his carved mice, but you'd be well advised to pick a quiet moment to search them all out.

But the Star has yet another asset, Mr and Mrs Dresser; he cooks and she runs the dining room. Once the neighbourhood converged on Harome only for its ploughing competitions; now it is more likely to make a straight furrow for Mr Dresser's menus, which for the past eleven years have been as consistent and as picturesque as the old thatched inn itself.

Piperade

A Basque dish made with peppers, onions, tomatoes, garlic and eggs.

1 red pepper (seeded and cut into small strips)
1 green pepper (seeded and cut into small strips)
1 lb of tomatoes (peeled and chopped)
2 medium onions (peeled and chopped)
2 cloves of garlic (crushed)
8 eggs
2 oz of butter
1 tablespoon of olive oil
Salt, freshly milled black pepper
Some parsley

Pre-heat the oven to 325°F (mark 3)

Heat half the butter with the olive oil in a flameproof casserole, then add the onions and crushed garlic and fry them gently for 10 minutes to soften. Next add the peppers and tomatoes, season with a little salt and freshly milled black pepper, and cook for a further 5 minutes. Then put a lid on the casserole and bake for 1½ hours. Beat the eggs and lightly season them. Place the casserole back on the top of the stove over a medium heat, add remaining butter then, using a wooden spoon, stir the liquid eggs in (just as you would for scrambled eggs) and keep stirring right round the edges of the pan. Remove from the heat while the eggs are still moist, pile into warmed serving dishes and sprinkle with fresh chopped parsley. *(Serves 4)*

Marinaded Pork with Calvados

2 pork fillets (1½ to 1¾ lb)
6 tablespoons of olive oil
4 tablespoons of lemon juice
1 crushed clove of garlic
2 fl. oz of Calvados
1 oz of butter
Salt, freshly milled black pepper

For the tomato sauce:
1 15-oz tin of Italian tomatoes
1 oz butter
1 medium onion (chopped small)
1 crushed clove of garlic
¼ teaspoon of crushed rosemary
¼ level teaspoon of sugar
Salt, freshly milled black pepper

Make up the marinade by mixing the olive oil, lemon juice, crushed garlic and some freshly milled black pepper together. Cut the pork fillets into slices about ½ inch thick. Pour the marinade over the pork fillet. Leave them in a cool place for 2 or 3 hours, turning them over now and then.

and hold it over the heat; when it is warm, set light to it and pour it into the pan, shaking and rotating until the flames die down. Then add the tomato sauce, bring to simmering point and simmer till the pork is cooked — about a further 10 minutes. (*Serves 4*)

Marjorie's Lemon Posset

A light, fluffy cold lemon soufflé mixture.

4 large eggs (separated)
3 large lemons (grated rind and juice)
6 oz of caster sugar
½ oz of powdered gelatine
¼ pint of double cream

Place the egg yolks in a basin with the sugar and finely grated rind and the juice from the lemons. Now put the bowl over a saucepan a quarter full of gently simmering water. Whisk the mixture (an electric whisk is best for this) until it's thick, pale and foamy — this will take about 10 minutes — then remove the bowl from the heat and continue whisking until the mixture has cooled. Soak the gelatine in 2 tablespoons of cold water for a minute or two (using an old cup), then place the cup in the hot water previously used and leave the gelatine to dissolve until completely transparent. Strain the gelatine into the lemon mixture, beat the cream until it just begins to thicken, and whisk the egg whites till stiff. Using a large metal spoon, carefully fold first the cream into the egg yolk mixture, then the whites — folding everything evenly together. Pour the mixture into individual serving dishes and chill thoroughly until firm before serving. (*Serves 4*)

Meanwhile make up the sauce by frying the onions gently in the butter for 10 minutes or so, then stir in the tomatoes and add the crushed garlic and rosemary. Season with freshly milled black pepper and salt, and add a little sugar to help bring out the flavour of the tomatoes. Cook the sauce over a gentle heat for half an hour, then press it through a sieve. To cook the pork, heat up 1 oz of butter in a large frying pan, add the pork slices plus the marinade and cook fiercely for 5 or 6 minutes until the slices are browned nicely all over. Now pour the Calvados into a ladle

130

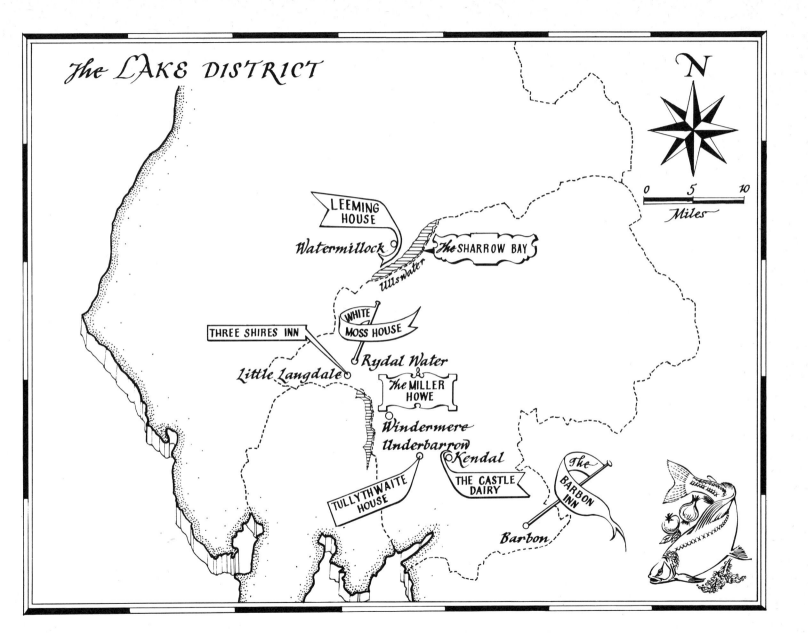

The LAKE DISTRICT

N

0   5   10
Miles

LEEMING HOUSE

Watermillock

The SHARROW BAY

Ullswater

WHITE MOSS HOUSE

THREE SHIRES INN

Rydal Water

Little Langdale

The MILLER HOWE

Windermere

Underbarrow

Kendal

TULLYTHWAITE HOUSE

THE CASTLE DAIRY

The BARBON INN

Barbon

Leeming House

Watermillock, Cumberland
Pooley Bridge 444

It is a reasonable bet, if you study Dorothy Wordsworth's Lakeland Journal, that it was the daffodils on this particular shore-line of Ullswater that inspired her brother. The beautiful twelve-acre landscaped garden of Leeming House wasn't laid out in his day, or he might have written a poem about that, too ('Ode to *Athrotaxis laxifolia*'). You can still contemplate the waves of daffodils, as well as a spectacular view of the lake, from one side of this late Georgian house. On the other, as you drive up to the impressive portico you are greeted by the relief of a hairy-looking but benevolent Viking. Watermillock is itself a corruption from the Norwegian – so this must be Ulla himself.

How appropriate, then, that a modern Norseman should have worked such wonders with this once derelict building. Just over four years ago Mr and Mrs Carlsen were literally camping out in it: today even 'Miss Elizabeth' (the kindly but meticulous resident ghost) would approve of the spacious elegance of their new hotel. Neither could she find any fault in chef Bob Burton's cooking, whose Roulage when we tasted it made us – never mind Wordsworth – quite lyrical.

Apple Soup à la Bourguignonne

1½ **pints of good all-purpose stock (see page 152)**
¾ **lb of cooking apples (peeled and coarsely chopped)**
1 **level teaspoon of ground ginger**
1 **egg yolk**
3 **tablespoons of double cream**
Salt, freshly milled black pepper
2 **oz of rice (cooked)**
1 **lemon (peeled, pith and pips removed, and cut in very thin slices)**

Strain the stock into a saucepan and bring to the boil. Add the coarsely chopped apples and simmer very gently without a lid till the apples are soft. Either press through a sieve or purée in an electric blender, then return the soup to the saucepan. Stir in the ground ginger, bring to simmering point and simmer for 5 minutes. Now beat the egg yolk and cream together in a basin. Take the soup off the heat, add a ladleful of soup to the cream

and egg mixture, mix thoroughly, then pour back into the soup and whisk. Check the seasoning, then pour into warmed soup bowls, sprinkle with warm cooked rice and serve immediately garnished with thin slices of lemon. (*Serves 6*)

Guinea-fowl with Juniper Berries

3 **guinea-fowl**
6 **oz of softened butter**
1 **Spanish onion (finely chopped)**
Juice of half a lemon
12 **juniper berries**
1 **level teaspoon of dried thyme**
Salt, freshly milled black pepper
1 **carrot, 1 onion, 1 stick of celery (all prepared)**
6 **peppercorns**
Small bunch of parsley
1 **pint of water**
¼ **pint of red Burgundy**
Beurre manié (see page 18, Canard en Casserole)

Prepare the guinea-fowl, removing the necks to make stock. Mix the softened butter with the finely chopped Spanish onion, lemon juice and dried thyme. Crush the juniper berries with the back of a tablespoon, and add to the butter mixture. Now thickly coat the breast of each bird with this mixture, place them in a shallow baking tin (about an inch deep) and leave them in a cool place for 2 hours. Meanwhile, make a strong stock by placing the necks of the birds and the vegetables, peppercorns, salt and parsley in a saucepan with a pint of water, and simmer gently for 1½ hours. To cook the birds place them in a pre-heated oven 425°F (mark 7), and roast for 20 to 25 minutes, basting frequently with the juices. The guinea-fowl are cooked when the juices run clear from the thickest part of the leg if this is pierced with a skewer.

The sauce is made by simmering ¾ pint of the strained stock with ¼ pint of Burgundy, thickened with beurre manié (1 oz flour and 1 oz butter) and seasoned to taste. When the birds are cooked, serve them cut into halves with the sauce poured over. (*Serves* 6)

Roulage au Chinois

For the sponge:
3 large eggs
4 oz of caster sugar
Finely grated rind of 1 orange
2 teaspoons of orange juice
3 oz of plain flour
½ level teaspoon of baking powder
2 level teaspoons of ground ginger
½ level teaspoon of ground cinnamon
¼ level teaspoon of salt
Icing sugar

For the filling:
½ pint of double cream
2 tablespoons of ginger marmalade
2 tablespoons of preserved ginger syrup
4 pieces of stem ginger (thinly sliced)

Pre-heat the oven to 375°F (mark 5).

Prepare a Swiss roll tin (13½ by 9½ inches) by oiling it, then line it with a suitably sized piece of greaseproof paper, pleating the corners to make it fit, and oil that. Break the eggs into a large bowl and whisk thoroughly, gradually adding the caster sugar, whisking till the mixture is thick enough to hold a trail when the whisk is lifted from the mix. Fold in the grated orange rind and juice then sift in the dry ingredients except the icing sugar and fold them in carefully using a metal spoon. Pour the mixture into the prepared tin and spread it out evenly using the back of a spoon. Bake the sponge for 15 to 20 minutes until the mixture is golden, well risen and beginning to shrink slightly from the edges of the tin. When it is cooked, allow it to cool in the tin, then have another piece of greaseproof paper the same size spread out on a flat surface and dusted liberally with sifted icing sugar. Turn the sponge out onto this and carefully peel off the greaseproof paper (which is now on the upper side). Lightly whip the cream with the marmalade, ginger syrup and sliced preserved ginger. Spread this all over the oblong sponge, then carefully roll it up like a Swiss roll – don't worry if the delicate sponge cracks a little here and there. Finally, dust the roll with more icing sugar and serve cut into thick slices. (*Serves* 6)

The Sharrow Bay

Ullswater, Cumberland
Pooley Bridge 301

When Francis Coulson and Brian Sack opened the Sharrow Bay twenty-five years ago as a tea shop (with only '£500, an Irish setter and a bicycle'), the Lake District was a gastronomic as well as a natural wilderness. Today it probably embraces more good cooking to the square mile than anywhere in England outside London – and that is partly their doing. The high standards they set

from the beginning, and maintained, have percolated to the other lakes. Mind you, never did anyone work harder to deserve such a reputation: Francis Coulson left us at midnight, after cooking all evening, to go and make the fresh croissants for breakfast!

The Sharrow Bay stands on the far side of Lake Ullswater by the water's edge (the far side, because the road only meanders round one bank). The hotel is intoxicating with the fragrance of flowers (one will even come as a gift with your meal), and the mountain views through the windows are quite breathtaking. You can readily

understand how it is the position that inspires Francis Coulson to such heights. As he says himself 'a light heart produces light cooking'.

Crème d'Or

A light carrot soup flavoured with orange.

¾ **pint of pure orange juice (unsweetened canned or bottled)**
1 **12½ oz tin of carrots (liquidised or sieved with their liquid)**
1 **orange (rind and juice)**
1½ **oz of butter**
1 **oz of flour**
1 **onion (chopped small)**
1 **clove of garlic (crushed)**
2 **level dessertspoons of sugar**
¼ **pint of chicken stock (home-made or from a cube)**
¼ **pint of double cream**
Salt, freshly milled black pepper

In a large thick saucepan gently melt the butter and fry the onion until it's transparent. Stir in the flour till smooth, then gradually add the stock, stirring well after each addition, and then the same with the liquidised carrots. Bring to simmering point, then add the garlic, grated orange rind and juice and the canned orange juice. Simmer gently for about 10 minutes, then add the sugar. Taste to check the seasoning and add salt and freshly milled black pepper if necessary. Sieve the soup and reheat gently. Finally stir in the cream and serve very hot. (*Serves 6*)

135

Allumettes de Boeuf

10 oz of made-up puff pastry
1 beaten egg
1½ lb of fillet steak (sinews and fat removed)
1½ level tablespoons of flour (seasoned with salt and cayenne pepper)
4 oz of butter
1 large onion (or preferably 3 small shallots) finely chopped
3 tablespoons of brandy
¼ pint of beef stock
½ pint of single cream
Freshly milled black pepper

Pre-heat the oven to 425°F (mark 7).

On a flat surface roll out the pastry to a 12-inch square, then cut out 8 rectangles measuring 3 inches by 6 inches. Lay 4 of these rectangles on a greased baking sheet; the other 4 rectangles should be marked with a ¾-inch wide border in from the edges and the centres cut out so that you now have 4 frames. Brush the pastry on the baking sheet with beaten egg, then fit a 'frame' over each rectangle and brush these with beaten egg. Now bake the pastry for 10 to 15 minutes or until it's well-risen and golden, then turn the heat off and leave cases in the oven to cool with the door slightly open. (These pastry cases can be prepared in advance, and need only to be warmed through before serving). To make the filling: take the fillet steak and cut it into matchstick strips, about 1 inch long, cutting down the fillet and not across the grain. Heat the butter in a wide, thick frying pan and gently cook the onion until soft. Toss the meat strips in seasoned flour,

turn up the heat, add the meat to the pan and cook it for 3 or 4 minutes, keeping it on the move with a wooden spoon so that it all cooks evenly (it's very important not to over-cook the meat – it must be pink inside). Now shake in a little more flour to soak up the juices in the pan, then heat the brandy in a small saucepan, pour it over the meat and set light to it (stand well back and shake the pan until the flames die down). Then gradually stir in the stock and the cream. Taste and season if necessary. Place the warmed pastry cases on heated plates (one per person), fill each one with the meat and sauce, and serve immediately. (*Serves 4*)

Brandy Angel Mousse

For the mousse:
3 large eggs
6 oz of caster sugar
3 tablespoons of brandy
2 tablespoons of rum
2 level teaspoons of gelatine powder (mixed
   with 2 tablespoons of warm water)
½ pint of double cream

For the decoration:
¼ pint of double cream
1 oz of flaked almonds

Separate the eggs and whisk the yolks and sugar together until thick and pale. Add the brandy and the rum and continue whisking for 2 or 3 minutes. Melt the soaked gelatine in a small cup over very hot water until it becomes completely clear, then strain it into the egg mixture and fold in. Beat the cream until thick, then do the same with the egg

whites until they form soft peaks when the whisk is lifted from the bowl. Now very, very gently fold the whipped cream, followed by the egg whites, into the egg yolk mixture. Spoon the mixture into stemmed glasses and chill thoroughly for 2 to 3 hours before serving. To serve, decorate with whipped cream and flaked almonds. (*Serves 4 or 6*)

The Barbon Inn

Barbon, Kirkby Lonsdale, Westmorland
Barbon 233

Roman legions once tramped through Barbon on their way to deal with the troublesome Picts, and in the eighteenth century the Sedbergh stage stopped regularly at this inn (which was a century old even then). But today the quiet of this peaceful village is disturbed by little more than the contented munching of diners at Mrs Blackmore-Moore's delightful inn. The food is the work of Margot Thurlby – Suzy, that is, to her friends – who stopped here on her way back to Australia and stayed for seventeen years. Perhaps it was curiosity that drove her to the kitchen – her mother, she says, was such a superb cook that no one else was allowed in. Anyway, we arrived at tea time.

Lord, what a do! Lemon cheese, scones and Cumberland rum butter, Guinness cake. It was hard enough lifting oneself out of the sofas under normal circumstances. But after that . . .

Cream of Watercress Soup

4 bunches of watercress
2 tablespoons of finely chopped onion
3 level tablespoons of butter
3 level tablespoons of flour
¾ pint of milk
¾ pint of chicken stock (see page 152)
4 fl. oz of double cream
2 egg yolks
1 teaspoon of fresh, chopped tarragon
1 tablespoon of freshly snipped chives
Salt, freshly milled black pepper and nutmeg

Wash the bunches of watercress, discarding any imperfect leaves and trimming off the stems, then chop the sprigs finely. Cook the onion gently in the butter until soft and just beginning to colour, stir in the flour and cook for 3 to 4 minutes, then add the milk bit by bit, stirring vigorously after each addition. Then add the watercress, tarragon and a grating of nutmeg. Stir gently over a low heat for 2 or 3 minutes, add the stock, stir again, taste and then add salt and freshly milled black pepper. Now pass the whole lot through a fine sieve into a double saucepan. Beat the egg yolks, add a ladleful of soup to them, stir and pour back into the soup, add the cream and stir till heated and slightly thickened. Serve the soup garnished with snipped chives. (*Serves 4*)

Sweetbreads in Cream and White Wine

1 lb of lambs' sweetbreads
1½ oz of butter
1 small onion (finely chopped)
2 level tablespoons of seasoned flour
2 level dessertspoons of flour
4 fl. oz of water
4 fl. oz of dry white wine
1 heaped tablespoon of chopped parsley
5 fl. oz of double cream
Salt, freshly milled black pepper

Pre-heat the oven to 325°F (mark 3)

Soak the sweetbreads in icy cold water for an hour, then put them in a saucepan with a fresh lot of water, bring to simmering point slowly and simmer gently for 15 minutes, drain and trim off any inedible bits, and put in another lot of icy cold water until completely cold. Drain again by pressing them first between two plates and then drying them thoroughly in absorbent paper. Roll the sweetbreads in seasoned flour and sauté them in a frying pan in butter till they are lightly coloured. Then using a draining spoon, transfer them to a casserole. Add a little more butter to the pan if it needs it, gently fry the onion to soften it, then stir in 2 dessertspoons of flour, blend well, then add the water a little at a time stirring, then do the same with the wine, season to taste and pour sauce over the sweetbreads, with some chopped parsley. Put a lid on the casserole, and cook slowly in the oven for an hour. Just before serving add the double cream, allow it to heat though without boiling, and serve. (*Serves 4*)

The Castle Dairy

Kendal, Westmorland
Kendal 21170

Even in the town noted for its ancient buildings, the Castle Dairy is a veteran. It was first built in the fourteenth century, as the dairy to Kendal Castle, whose most famous occupant was Katherine Parr, one of the luckier wives of Henry VIII. When the castle fell into disrepair and its handsome deer departed, the dairy passed to a stonemason who did it up as his own house in 1566. And so it remains today, a perfect Tudor house, down to the squint windows and the blackbird ledge (where they were encouraged to nest, so they could finish up in a pie).

Inside it is anything but a lifeless relic from the past: the kettle sings on the Victorian range, and, cook and hostess respectively, Avril Leigh and Elaine Wright have merrily brought the timbered rooms back to life. They enjoy, they say, a relaxed and comfortable life themselves, and like nothing better than spreading goodwill at dinner time. The food is worthy of the hospitality; we arrived at lunchtime, when the restaurant is closed, but the 'coffee and sandwiches' turned out to be a magnificent four-course lunch, most of which we can pass on in our own way below; the Château Latour '44 you must imagine for yourselves, I'm afraid.

Peasant Soup

2 oz of butter
2 large carrots (sliced)
2 large onions (sliced)
2 large leeks, white parts only (sliced)
2 large tomatoes (skinned and sliced)
1 small turnip (sliced)
2 whole cloves
2 pints of stock
3 tablespoons of chopped parsley
4 tablespoons of double cream
Salt, freshly milled black pepper
6 whole peppercorns

In a large saucepan melt the butter, then stir in all the vegetables and stir them round and round until all are nice and buttery. Keeping the heat low, put a lid on the saucepan and let the vegetables 'sweat' for 15 minutes (stirring them round a couple of times during this). Now add the parsley, cloves, the whole peppercorns and a seasoning of salt. Pour the stock in, put the lid back on and simmer gently for 20 to 25 minutes, or until the vegetables are quite soft. Then press the whole lot through a large sieve, extracting

the cloves and peppercorns. Pour back into the saucepan to reheat, taste to check seasoning and stir in the cream just before serving. (*Serves 6*)

Venison Cooked in Clay

A joint of venison (3 ½ to 4 lb)
1 level dessertspoon of powdered ginger
1 medium onion, studded with about 8 cloves
1 oz of butter and
1 oz of flour mixed to a paste

Pre-heat the oven to 350°F (mark 4).

Prepare the joint by wiping it and rubbing it all over with powdered ginger. If you've got or can get hold of a clay cooking pot (for example, a Roman cooking pot, a large oblong terracotta pot with a domed lid or a large-sized chicken brick) rinse the inside out with water to dampen the clay slightly, place the joint in it accompanied by an onion stuck with cloves. Put the lid on and cook for 2 ½ hours, or until tender, in the oven.
Alternatively, you can place the joint in a large piece of foil together with the onion etc., sprinkle a tablespoon of water over it, and seal up into a neat, fairly loose parcel. Place in a large casserole, put the lid on and cook for 2 ½ to 3 hours. Either way, when the joint is cooked, remove it to a warmed serving dish, keep warm, then pour all the juices that have come out during the cooking into a saucepan. Add a few peanut-sized pieces of butter and flour paste (beurre manié) to them, and stir over a low heat till thickened. Carve the meat and pour the sauce over. (*Serves 6 or 8*)

Border Pasty

Shortcrust pastry:
10 oz of flour
A pinch of salt
2 ½ oz of lard
2 ½ oz of butter or margarine

Rum butter filling:
4 oz of unsalted butter
2 ½ oz of light soft brown sugar
The grated rind of 1 small lemon
1 ½ tablespoons of rum
¼ level teaspoon of ground cinnamon
1 lb of currants
Milk and sugar to glaze

Pre-heat the oven to 425°F (mark 7).

Make the pastry, and then the rum butter as follows. In a bowl beat the softened butter till light and fluffy, beat in the sugar bit by bit, followed by the cinnamon and grated lemon rind. Finally beat in the rum a few drops at a time. Combine with the currants. Roll out half the pastry to line a 10-inch enamel pie plate, and use the trimmings to make an extra border round the edge. Spread the filling over the pastry base. Roll out the remaining pastry, dampen the edges of the pie, place the pastry lid over the filling and seal well all round by pinching or fluting the edges. Brush the top with milk, make a few snips with the ends of some scissors, sprinkle with more soft brown sugar, and bake for 25 to 30 minutes. This can be eaten hot or cold, but we think it's nicest served warm with thick cream. (*Serves 6 or 8*)

local tannery until in 1800 some very up-to-date occupants altered it and designated it The Modern Villa – the sitting room still contains a fine Adam sideboard fitted into its own alcove. Mrs Johnson describes herself as 'a plain English cook', but that is an injustice. Anyone who has eaten with her in the past thirty-three years, here or at Hodge Hill, would say it was English food not at its plainest, but at its most imaginative.

Fresh Salmon and Cucumber Mousse

6 oz of fresh cold salmon (cooked and finely mashed)
3 level teaspoons of powdered gelatine
¼ pint of boiling water
¼ pint of fresh single cream
The yolks and whites of 2 eggs
1 level teaspoon of paprika
½ level teaspoon of salt
1 tablespoon of lemon juice
2 tablespoons of peeled cucumber (chopped into smallish dice)
A few thin slices of cucumber for decoration

Start by bringing the water to the boil in a small saucepan, gradually sprinkling in the powdered gelatine and stirring well until dissolved; then set aside. Now warm the cream slightly and then beat it into the egg yolks thoroughly. Next stir in the dissolved gelatine and add the salt, paprika and lemon juice. The mixture should now be allowed to get quite cold and when it's just beginning to set, the mashed salmon and cucumber should

Tullythwaite House

Underbarrow, Westmorland
Crosthwaite 397

Mrs Johnson, who runs this peaceful guesthouse a few miles out of Kendal, is the great lady of the Lakes. That is the verdict of many of the fine cooks to be found in this epicurean corner of England; it is in her dining room that they eat on their night off, and they are (she says) her 'little chicks'. With such testimonials, it's perhaps as well that Tullythwaite House is so secluded. With a view as serene as it is unpopulated, it stands in twenty-four acres farmed by Mrs Johnson's son (who also married a good cook) – so it never lacks for its own milk and dairy produce.

It was built in 1636, and served as the

be stirred in. Next beat the egg whites until stiff and carefully fold them in. Spoon the mixture into 4 large wine glasses and chill thoroughly until firm. Just before serving, decorate each one with thin slices of cucumber. (*Serves 4*)

Loin of Lamb with Green Pepper Stuffing, Orange, Redcurrant and Mint Sauce

1 loin of lamb, boned, rolled and tied (ask the butcher to do this for you)
2 small green peppers
2 small onions
3 oz of butter or margarine
4 oz of freshly made white breadcrumbs
2 teaspoons of finely grated lemon rind
1 level teaspoon of salt
Freshly milled black pepper
2 standard eggs
A small glass of red wine
4 tablespoons of Wilkie & Sons Tiptree red-currant jelly
Grated rind of 1 largish orange
1½ tablespoons of freshly chopped mint

First make the stuffing: cut the peppers in half, remove the seeds and the pith, place them in a saucepan of cold water, then bring them to the boil. Drain and chop them very finely. Now peel and finely chop the onions, melt the butter in a small saucepan and gently cook the onions in it for 5 minutes. Remove from the heat and stir in the chopped peppers, breadcrumbs, grated lemon peel and a good seasoning of salt and pepper. Allow the mixture to cool slightly, then lightly beat the eggs and stir them into the mixture. Now take

a dollop of it and roll it into a ball between the palms of your hands – and do likewise with the rest (a sticky operation, but worth it).

The loin of lamb should be placed in a roasting tin and roasted in a pre-heated oven (400°F (mark 6)) for about 1 to 1¼ hours depending on how you like it. During the last 20 minutes of the cooking time, spoon off most of the fat and place the little balls of stuffing round the meat. To serve, place the joint on a serving dish surrounded by the stuffing. Make a little gravy by spooning off all the fat from the meat juices, adding a small glass of red wine to the pan and letting it bubble and reduce a bit over a strong heat.

Finally, make the sauce. Place the jelly in a small basin and break it up with a fork, then add the orange rind and the mint. Beat with a fork to amalgamate everything, and hand it round separately with the lamb. (*Serves 6*)

Hazelnut Meringue Gâteau with Chocolate Sauce

For the meringue:
8 egg whites
1 lb of caster sugar

For the filling:
4 oz of caster sugar
3 egg yolks
¼ pint of milk
½ lb of unsalted butter
4 oz of toasted hazelnuts
1 tablespoon of sherry
½ pint of double cream
Chocolate sauce

Start by lining 2 baking sheets with non-

stick parchment paper and drawing a 10-inch circle on each one. Turn the oven on to 275°F (mark 1).

In a very large mixing bowl beat egg whites until stiff, then add half the sugar and whisk again until really stiff. Carefully fold in the remaining sugar. Use half the mixture to fill each circle, drawing the meringue out to the edge with a palette knife in each case. Dry the meringues in the oven for about 3 hours or until they're crisp and firm, then allow to cool and carefully peel off the paper.

To make the filling, cream the sugar and egg yolks until pale and creamy, warm the milk, stir it into the egg yolk mixture, then pour the whole lot into a double saucepan with hot water in the bottom half. Cook over a low heat until the mixture thickens and well coats the back of a spoon. Do not let the mixture boil.

Now cream the butter until fluffy, gradually beat in the cooled (but not cold) egg mixture and continue beating until the mixture is light and fluffy. The hazelnuts should be ground or minced (reserve 12 whole nuts for the decoration). Stir the ground nuts into the butter mixture along with the sherry; use this mixture to sandwich the two meringues together. One hour before serving, whip the cream until it *just* holds its shape – be careful not to overwhip it. Then spoon it into a forcing bag with a 1-inch star nozzle, and pipe whirls of cream on top of the gâteau, and top each whirl of cream with a hazelnut. Keep the gâteau in a cool place, and serve with chocolate sauce handed round separately.

(Note: this can be made for 6 people using half quantities (2 small egg yolks) and drawing smaller circles for the meringue.) (*Serves 12*)

Three Shires Inn

Little Langdale, Near Ambleside, Westmorland
Langdale 215

Deep in the Fells, three counties (Lancashire, Cumberland and Westmorland) come together. And they could hardly pick a better spot to meet than at Mr and Mrs Poole's inn. Stone-built and sturdy outside, comforting and cosy within, it has stood first as a beer-house, then as a posting-stage for almost exactly a century on the only pass that links the

Lakes with the coast at Ravenglass. Hikers, rather than smugglers and quarrymen, today trudge up or around Wetherlam, the dominating local peak in a wilderness of peaks – and you can take it that Mrs Poole sees to it that they leave The Three Shires armed with something a lot better than the jam butties which long ago gave their name to Jam Street further down the hill. The fame of Mrs Poole's cooking is spread a great deal further than just three shires. In such surroundings it isn't perhaps surprising to find her championing genuine old English cooking, but there are few other places where you'd find such an admirable exponent of it.

Smoked Haddock Mousse

1 lb of smoked haddock
½ pint of milk
½ oz of powdered gelatine
½ pint of mayonnaise
¼ pint of double cream (lightly whipped)
The juice of 1 lemon
2 hard-boiled eggs (finely chopped)
Freshly milled black pepper
Butter
Flour

Pre-heat the oven to 350°F (mark 4).

Place the fish in a shallow baking dish, season with pepper, pour the milk over it and bake in the oven for about 20 minutes. Then, reserving the cooking liquid, remove the bones and skin and flake the fish. Now, using

about ¾ oz of flour and 1 oz of butter, make up a sauce with the cooking liquid.

Dissolve the gelatine in the lemon juice, placing it in a cup sitting in a pan of barely-simmering water (it's ready when it has turned absolutely transparent). Now beat the cream lightly until it begins to thicken. Next put the white sauce, the mayonnaise and flaked fish into the liquidiser and blend till smooth. Turn the mixture out into a bowl, then blend in the melted gelatine and fold in the whipped cream followed by the hard-boiled eggs. Add a bit more pepper if it needs it, spoon the mixture into 6 individual ramekin dishes and chill till firm and set. Serve garnished with sprigs of watercress. (*Serves 6*)

Chicken with Apples and Cider

2 small (3-lb) chickens
2 carrots, 1 onion, cloves, parsley stalks
2 large onions
½ lb of mushrooms
1 clove of garlic
2 slices of gammon
4 large baking apples
Stock
Salt, paprika and freshly milled black pepper
Flour (for thickening)
Butter and oil (for frying)
1 pint of sweet cider

Cook the chickens first: place them in a large casserole with 2 chopped carrots, an onion stuck with 4 to 5 cloves, seasoning and a few parsley stalks; just cover them with water and simmer gently for around 45 minutes, or until tender. Reserve the stock.

Take off the chicken flesh, keeping the pieces fairly large.

In a very large pan, fry the onions and the garlic gently in butter and oil, then add the gammon (cut into small cubes), the mushrooms (sliced) and the apples (sliced). Cook these for a minute or two, and add freshly milled black pepper and a little paprika but no salt at this stage because of the gammon. Now sprinkle in 2 tablespoons of flour, stirring it well into everything, then add the cider gradually and about ½ pint of the chicken stock. Reheat and simmer very gently for about 10 minutes; add the chicken pieces and reheat gently for a further 10 minutes – without letting it come to the boil. Taste to check the seasoning, and serve with rice and a green salad. (*Serves 8*)

Spotted Dick with Syrup Sauce

8 oz of self-raising flour
1 pinch of salt
4 oz of butter (room temperature)
2 oz of caster sugar
**6 oz of sultanas or currants (washed) or half
  and half**
2 eggs, and a little milk
3 tablespoons of golden syrup

Sift flour and salt into a basin, then rub in butter till the mixture looks like fine crumbs, and stir in the sugar and dried fruit. Beat the eggs and add them to the mixture, stirring till smooth with a wooden spoon; add a little milk to give a good dropping consistency. Put this mixture into a well-buttered 2-pint pudding basin, cover with a sheet of grease-proof paper and a sheet of foil, making a pleat in the centre to allow for expansion. Tie up securely with string and steam in a steamer over simmering water for 2 to 3 hours. Serve with a hot syrup sauce, made simply by melting some golden syrup in a saucepan and taking to the table very hot. (*Serves 4*)

White Moss House

Rydal Water, Grasmere, Westmorland
Grasmere 295

Wordsworth 'owned' so many houses in the Lake District that it's almost incredible to find one which really did belong to him. A framed document in the hall of White Moss House proclaims this to be indisputably so. In those days it was two cottages which, in 1830, for the princely sum of 'five shillings of lawful money' he sold to his son, the contract to be complete at the end of the year 'for the rent of one peppercorn'. Another framed deed declares that a hundred years ago the house was entitled to its private water supply for half a crown a year: it still costs 12½p, which shows you can beat inflation sometimes.

Much else is genuine in this early eighteenth-century house overlooking Rydal Water – not least Mrs Butterworth's genuine and inspired English cooking. For anyone who believes that a feeling for food is an inherited gift, it will come as no surprise that Mrs Butterworth's grandmother was a cook in a big house. She remembers her Gran making this first recipe in the fire oven, at the end of baking day so that the heat was very low, then serving it with freshly made buttered muffins for high tea.

Lancashire Cheese and Onions

½ lb of onions
6 oz of Lancashire cheese
¼ pint of milk
1 level dessertspoon of cornflour
Freshly grated nutmeg and seasoning

Peel and chop the onions and place them in a casserole; barely cover with water and bake uncovered in a slow oven (300°F (mark 2)) till soft but not coloured – this will take 1½ to 2 hours. When the onions are soft, mix the cornflour with a little of the milk until smooth, then add the rest of the milk and pour this mixture on to the onion, together with the crumbled cheese. Return the casserole to the oven until the cheese has melted, taste and season if necessary, and serve with freshly grated nutmeg on top. (*Serves 4*)

Beef and Red Wine Pie

1¼ lb of best stewing steak
¼ lb of ox kidney
1 tablespoon of finely chopped onion
1 tablespoon of finely chopped fresh marjoram
Salt, freshly milled black pepper
½ pint of dry red wine
A little beef dripping
1 level tablespoon of flour
A little beaten egg
8 oz shortcrust pastry (see below)

Trim and cut the steak and kidney into smallish pieces, then put them into a bowl, cover with the onion and marjoram and season with salt and freshly milled black pepper. Pour in

the red wine and turn the meat around, cover and leave in a cool place (for example the lowest part of the refrigerator) overnight. Next day drain the meat thoroughly, melt some dripping in a large saucepan and when it's hot, fry the meat to seal in the juices. Now sprinkle the flour over the meat, stir well and gradually add the marinade and a bit more seasoning. Put a lid on and simmer very gently for about 1½ to 2 hours or until the meat is tender.

Meanwhile make the pastry with 8 oz of plain flour, a pinch of salt, and a 4-oz block of margarine taken straight from the refrigerator and grated into the flour. Stir lightly and mix

with iced water to form a very soft dough. Let the pastry rest in a cold place for ½ an hour before using.

Allow the meat mixture to cool, then turn it into a 1½ pint oval pie dish, put the pastry lid on, decorate with leaves made from the trimmings and brush with beaten egg. Bake in a pre-heated oven (450°F (mark 8)) for 25 minutes.

Sticky Oatmeal Parkin

½ lb of medium oatmeal
¼ lb of self-raising flour
½ lb of black treacle
5 oz of lard
2 oz of dark soft brown sugar
1 level teaspoon of ground ginger
½ level teaspoon of bicarbonate of soda
½ level teaspoon of salt
½ teacup of milk and 1 egg (whisked together)

Pre-heat the oven to 325°F (mark 3).

First melt the lard and treacle together in a saucepan, and mix the soda with the milk mixture. Sift remaining ingredients into a bowl, make a well in the centre and add the syrup mixture then the milk mixture. Mix very thoroughly using a wooden spoon. Pour into a greased, lined loaf tin (about 9 inches by 6 inches by 2 inches) and bake for 1½ to 2 hours.

This was originally a Northern teatime cake, but it makes a good sweet course at a family meal, topped with stewed apples and served with cream. Parkin also improves with keeping if stored in an airtight tin for a few days – if you can wait that long!

The Miller Howe

Windermere, Westmorland
Windermere 2536

A Windermere sunset at its best is an epic theatrical event, and the Miller Howe, perched up above the eastern bank of the lake, has a dress circle view of it. Little wonder then that John Tovey, with a theatrical background himself, should make the most of it, especially when the performance coincides with his magnificent dinner. The audience is assembled for 8.30. Backstage in the kitchen the call is for 'beginners, please!'. The houselights dim, and there through the proscenium window of the dining room the sun hovers above Crinkle Crags, then sinks perceptibly behind Scafell Pike (this whole drama you can follow on your menu, which illustrates the panorama before you).

And that is only the overture, for a virtuoso dinner follows in five acts. Then you understand how it is that within two years of opening John Tovey is packing them in every night. You'd never believe he had not cooked professionally before, so prodigious is his range and inventiveness (a *Times* article on sorrel soup, he says, is what started him off). At the Miller Howe every night is a first night.

Cold Leeks with Carrot, Tomato and Soured Cream

8 medium leeks
1 medium onion
4 slices of fresh root ginger
½ pint of soured cream
4 small carrots
4 medium tomatoes
1 good pinch of English mustard powder
4 large lettuce leaves
French dressing
4 sprigs of watercress
4 twists of orange peel
Salt, freshly milled black pepper

Pre-heat the oven to 350°F (mark 4).

Trim the leeks, removing the tough outer layers and leaving about ½ inch of the green part, then split them in half lengthways and wash in several changes of cold water to remove any dirt and grit. Half-fill a roasting tin with water, to which a chopped onion and the 4 slices of root ginger should be added. Then fit a wire rack or wire cooling tray in or onto the roasting tin. Now place the leek halves together again, put them side by side on the wire rack and season with salt

and freshly milled black pepper. Cover with foil and bake in the oven for 1 hour or until the leeks are quite tender. To make the sauce, peel the tomatoes, quarter them and press them through a sieve to extract the pips. To the tomato pulp, add the 4 carrots (grated), then stir in the soured cream together with a generous pinch of mustard. When the leeks are cool, arrange them on French-dressed lettuce leaves, pour the sauce over and garnish with sprigs of watercress and twists of orange peel. (Serves 4)

Spring Cabbage Baked in Oil and Garlic with Juniper Berries

1½ to 2 lb of spring cabbage
1 onion (finely chopped)
2 cloves of garlic (very finely chopped)
6 juniper berries
Salt, freshly milled black pepper
Olive oil

Pre-heat the oven to 400°F (mark 6).

Remove the tough outer leaves of the cabbage and discard them, selecting only the good green leaves. Remove the centres of these, then very finely shred the cabbage, wash well in a colander and dry thoroughly in a clean cloth or some kitchen paper. Take a small flameproof casserole, pour in enough olive oil to just cover the bottom and gently fry the onion and garlic in it till pale gold, then stir in the cabbage and the juniper berries (which should be crushed finely in a pestle and mortar, or with the back of a tablespoon), plus a seasoning of salt and freshly milled

black pepper. Stir to get everything glistening with oil, then put a tight lid on and bake in the oven for 35 minutes by which time the cabbage will be cooked, but not too much – still nice and crisp. (Serves 4 to 6)

Rum and Black Cherry Pie

For the pastry:
6 oz of self-raising flour
2 oz of cornflour
2 oz of caster sugar
1 egg yolk
The grated rind of ½ lemon
6 oz of butter (softened)

For the filling:
1½ lb of black cherries
3 level tablespoons of demerara sugar
2 tablespoons of rum
½ level teaspoon of ground cinnamon

In a large deep bowl crumb together the (sifted) self-raising flour and cornflour into the butter (don't apply great pressure – just gently lift up high and drop back into the bowl). When the mixture is crumbed, add the caster sugar and grated lemon rind and mix thoroughly. Beat the egg yolk lightly and sprinkle over the dry contents of the bowl, then shake the bowl (as if 'panning for gold' Mr Tovey suggests – this gently brings the flour, fat and egg together, forming larger and larger nuts). Then move your hand round the inside of the bowl and scoop the mixture, bringing it together. Leave to rest in the refrigerator for about ½ an hour – it will in fact keep for 4 to 5 days if needed – then remove and bring up to room temperature again.

Now wash the cherries, and half-cook them gently together with the sugar, rum and cinnamon for about 5 or 6 minutes, then pile them into a 1½-pint oval pie dish. Top with pastry, make a few slits in the centre and bake for 25 to 30 minutes 425°F (mark 7). (*Serves 6*)

Orange Mousse

3 large eggs
2 egg yolks
3 oz of caster sugar
½ oz of powdered gelatine
3 tablespoons of water
2 tablespoons of orange Curaçao
½ pint of double cream
1 can of frozen orange juice (6 fl. oz – thawed)
2 oranges (juice and grated rind)

Break the whole eggs and the egg yolks into a mixing bowl, and put the gelatine, water and orange Curaçao in a small basin to soak, then place over a pan of hot water to melt. Now, using an electric whisk if possible, whisk the eggs, adding the sugar a little at a time, and continue whisking until the eggs and sugar form a ribbon (in other words, when you take the whisk out and write the letter M in the mixture, the start of the upward stroke is still visible when you come to the end of the downward stroke). Whisk the cream till it just holds its shape, then fold in the thawed orange juice, plus the fresh orange juice and grated rind. Now strain the melted gelatine (which should be absolutely clear) into the egg yolk mixture, then fold in the cream and orange juice mixture. Pour into individual ramekins or stemmed glasses and chill thoroughly before serving. (*Serves 8*)

Basic Recipes for Reference

Homemade Mayonnaise

2 large egg yolks
½ pint of olive oil
1 level teaspoon of mustard powder
1 or 2 teaspoons of white wine vinegar
Salt, freshly milled black pepper

If you've never made mayonnaise, I suggest you start with a good groundnut oil, which is less expensive to practise on than olive oil. However, when you come to using olive oil (which is essential for a really good mayonnaise) it's important to use a brand you know you like. I personally find that very strong-tasting virgin oil or first pressings are too overpowering for mayonnaise, so I like to use a mild olive oil (but it's really up to you to decide which you like the best).

Place a 1½-pint pudding basin on a damp tea towel to keep it steady, place the egg yolks in it with the mustard, a little salt and some freshly milled black pepper (if you don't like seeing black speckles of pepper in mayonnaise, you can of course use white). An electric hand whisk would be ideal for the mixing, but an ordinary balloon whisk will do if you're prepared to put a bit of effort into it. Put the oil in a jug and have the vinegar to hand.

First whisk the egg yolks very thoroughly, then using a teaspoon add one drop of olive oil and beat that in. Then add another drop and whisk that in (it seems very tedious but the results are well worth it). Continue adding your drops, and when it starts to thicken, you can start adding bigger drops and finally quite large splodges. When half the oil is in it will have become very thick, so that you then add a teaspoon of wine vinegar. As you are now past danger point, you can keep the whisk going continuously and pour in the rest of the oil in a thin steady stream, until you have a pale thick shiny sauce. At the end taste to check the seasoning, and add a little more vinegar if you think it needs it.

Store the mayonnaise in a screw-top jar. When made by the above method, I find it keeps in the lowest part of the refrigerator for up to a week with no ill effects. If it curdles – and it *will* if the oil is added too quickly at the beginning – start again with a new egg yolk and add the curdled mixture drop by drop.

To make *garlic mayonnaise*: add 1 or 2 crushed cloves of garlic right at the beginning of the whole procedure. (*Serves 4*)

Homemade Tomato Sauce

1 lb of firm ripe tomatoes (peeled and chopped)
1 small onion (finely chopped)
1 teaspoon of fresh chopped basil *or*
½ level teaspoon of dried basil
½ level teaspoon of caster sugar
Salt, freshly milled black pepper
Oil and butter

Melt a little oil and butter in a thick saucepan, and gently sauté the onion in it for 5 minutes, then add the tomatoes, basil, sugar and a seasoning of salt and freshly milled black pepper. Stir well and simmer for 25 to 30 minutes, then press through a fine sieve to extract the pips etc. Reheat and serve. (*Serves 4*)

Sauce Hollandaise

4 egg yolks from large eggs
5 oz of salted butter (room temperature)
2 tablespoons of dry white wine
4 peppercorns
5 tablespoons (approx) of water
1 teaspoon of lemon juice

Put the wine, 3 tablespoons of water and the peppercorns into a small saucepan and boil till reduced by half. Now fill the bottom half of a double boiler with cold water, and put the reduced liquid (minus the peppercorns) into the top half. Add another tablespoon of cold water and turn the heat underneath to medium. Beat the egg yolks well, then pour them into the boiler, whisk them with a balloon whisk and when they are frothy, start to add the butter – about a teaspoonful at a time – whisking all the while. Be careful not to let the water underneath reach boiling point (turn the heat down if necessary). When all the butter is whisked in and the sauce is thickened, add another tablespoon of cold water and a teaspoon of lemon juice. The sauce is now ready; to keep warm, leave it sitting over the hot water. (*Serves 4 or 6*)

Quick Espagnole Sauce

1 rasher of fat streaky bacon (diced)
2 level tablespoons of butter
1 large Spanish onion (coarsely chopped)
2 medium carrots (coarsely chopped)
1 stalk of celery
1 bay leaf
1/4 level teaspoon of dried thyme
3 level tablespoons of flour
1 level tablespoon of tomato paste
3/4 pint of beef stock
5 or 6 tablespoons of dry white wine or
sherry
Salt, freshly milled black pepper

Heat the butter in a saucepan and sauté the diced bacon until transparent. Then add the coarsely chopped vegetables and the herbs and continue to cook over a moderate heat until the vegetables are well browned all over. Now sprinkle the vegetables with flour, lower the heat and continue to sauté, stirring, for 2 to 3 minutes or until the flour is a rich golden colour. Stir the tomato paste into the mixture, then gradually add the stock and wine, still stirring constantly. Bring the sauce to the boil, then simmer for about 20 minutes with the saucepan lid half on, stirring occasionally. Then press the sauce through a fine sieve and season to taste with salt and freshly milled black pepper. (You may have to adjust the consistency of the sauce with 2 or 3 tablespoons of water – it depends on how long or how vigorously the sauce has been cooked.) Use immediately or store in the refrigerator till needed. These quantities make about 3/4 pint.

Caramel Sauce

1 lb of granulated sugar
1/2 pint of boiling water
A squeeze of lemon juice

Place the sugar in a large heavy saucepan, and then melt it over a moderate heat, stirring all the time, until the liquid formed is dark brown and the sugar itself has completely melted. Immediately, but slowly, add the boiling water (the mixture will tend to splutter, so be prepared to stand well back). Bring the mixture back to the boil again, stirring, then remove from the heat, add a squeeze of lemon juice and leave to cool.

Homemade All-Purpose Stock

1 1/2 lb of marrow bones (chopped)
1 lb leg of beef (cut in chunks)
2 beef stock cubes
3 pints of water
1 large carrot (roughly chopped)
1 onion (sliced)
1 stick of celery
1 small bunch of parsley
1 small bunch of celery tops
1 bay leaf
1 level teaspoon of dried mixed herbs
Salt, a few peppercorns

Place the meat and bones in a roasting tin and bake in a hot oven for 20 minutes or so to brown. Pour off any excess fat, then place them in a stockpot with all the other ingredients. Bring to simmering point, skim the surface, then simmer with a lid on for 4 hours. Strain the stock, and when cool remove the fat from the surface. This stock will keep for 2 or 3 days in a refrigerator.

Chicken Stock

The neck, gizzard, heart and any scraps (e.g. parson's nose, wing tips, etc)
1 onion (cut into chunks)
1 carrot (cut into chunks)
3/4 pint of chicken stock from a cube
2 sprigs of parsley
1 small bay leaf
1 sprig of thyme

Chop the chicken parts into 1-inch pieces, and place them in a saucepan with all the other ingredients and enough water to cover the contents to a depth of 1/2 an inch. Half cover the saucepan with the lid and simmer for a minimum of 1 hour, skimming the liquid whenever necessary. Strain the stock, skim the fat from the surface, and use as required.

Fish Stock

1 lb of fish trimmings (e.g. bones, skin, head, shells, etc.)
1 small onion (roughly chopped)
1 small carrot (roughly chopped)
1 stick of celery (roughly chopped)
2 or 3 whole button mushrooms
A strip of lemon rind
The juice of 1 small lemon
3 sprigs of parsley
A little salt
6 black peppercorns
1/4 pint of dry white wine
2 pints of cold water

Place all the ingredients together in a saucepan and bring to simmering point. Remove any surface scum, then simmer gently (uncovered) for 30 minutes. Pour the contents of the saucepan into a sieve lined with kitchen paper, and use the strained stock as required.

To clean Mussels

As soon as you get them home, put them into a sinkful of cold water. Throw out any that float to the top, then leave the cold tap running on the remainder for 15 minutes or so. Then take a small knife, scrape off all the barnacles, and pull off the little hairy beards. Discard any mussels that are broken and any that are open and refuse to close tight with a sharp tap from the knife. (In fact, the fresher the mussels, the tighter closed the shells will be – so watch out for gaping mussels when you're buying them.)
After you've cleaned each one, put it straight into another bowl or bucket of cold water. When they're all in, swirl them around in 3 or 4 more changes of water to get rid of every bit of grit or sand. Leave them covered in cold water until you're ready to cook them.

Croûtons

Cut some stale bread into small cubes. Melt some oil and butter in a thick-based frying pan, and when hot fry the cubes of bread a few at a time till crisp on all sides. Drain on kitchen paper and serve sprinkled with chopped parsley.

Garlic Croûtons

Larger croûtons can be made by oiling a baking tray and rubbing it with a clove of garlic. Thinly slice a stale French loaf in slightly diagonal slices, arrange them on the oiled tin and bake in a slow oven (325°F (mark 3)) until golden brown and crisp. These can be stored in an airtight container and are most useful for serving with pâtés, etc., instead of toast.

Batter for Crêpes or Pancakes

4 oz of plain flour
A pinch of salt
2 large fresh eggs
7 fl. oz of milk and
3 fl. oz of water mixed together
2 tablespoons of melted butter, unsalted
**   approx. 1 oz)**

Sift the flour and salt into a largish mixing bowl, then make a well in the centre and break the 2 eggs into it. Now start to whisk the eggs, incorporating bits of flour from the edges. Add a drop of milk-and-water from time to time and ignore the lumps – they'll all disappear later. When all the milk has been slowly added to the eggs and flour, give everything a thorough whisking (with an electric hand-mixer, or else a rotary or balloon whisk). When the batter is frothy and bubbly and all the lumps have vanished, it's ready and should be of the consistency of thin cream. Finally, stir in the melted butter just before cooking the pancakes.

Meringue Round (for Pavlova, etc.)

3 large fresh egg whites
6 oz of caster sugar
1 level teaspoon of cornflour
½ teaspoon of vinegar

Pre-heat the oven to gas mark 2 (300°F)

Prepare a baking sheet by oiling it and lining with greaseproof paper (and oil that slightly). Now whisk the egg whites until they form soft peaks, then whisk in the sugar – approximately 1 oz at a time. When all the sugar is in, whisk in the cornflour and vinegar, then spoon the meringue mixture onto the baking sheet, forming a round about 8 inches in diameter. Place the baking sheet in the oven, turn down the heat to gas mark 1 (275°F) and let the meringue round cook for 1 hour. Now turn the heat off, but leave the meringue inside the oven until this is quite cold; this operation dries it out beautifully. Peel the paper away from the base of the meringue, place on a serving dish and use as required.

General Index

See also Classified Index (*page 158*) for entries grouped under headings such as 'Soups', 'Fish', 'Meat', etc.
For a complete list of the inns and restaurants, see the Contents (page 6) at the beginning of the book.

Agneau Bédouin, 51
    Catalane, 59
Alaska Flambé, Baked, 117
Almond and Apple Pudding, 39
  and Celery Soup, 51
  and Coffee Tart, 61
All-Purpose Stock, Home-made, 152
Allumettes de Boeuf, 136
  de Porc à la Crème, 79
Amaretti Schokoladentorte, 127
Anchovy Sauce, 83
Angel Mousse, Brandy, 137
Apple and Almond Pudding, 39
  and Blackberry Meringue, 87
  and Hazelnut Galette, 91
  Soup à la Bourguignonne, 133
Apricot Sauce: see Fillet of Pork, 75
  Stuffing: see Leg of Lamb, 15
Armenian Lamb Pilaff, 71
  Mushrooms, 16
Artichokes, Globe, 34
Aubergine(s) Fritters with Tomato and Tarragon
    Sauce, 28
  Stuffed, 48
Austrian Braised Red Cabbage, 63
Avocado, Baked, 84
Avgolemono, 46

Baked Alaska Flambé, 117
  Avocado with Walnut Butter, 84
  Codling, 15
  Spring Cabbage, 149
Banana and Ginger Meringue Cake, 15
  and Peach Pudding, 96
  Créole, 77
Barbecued Pork Fillet with Fried Rice, 49
Baskets, Raspberry Meringue, 79
Batter for Crêpes or Pancakes, 153
Bédouin Lamb, 51
Beef Allumettes, 136
  and Red Wine Pie, 147
  Bourguignonne, 107
  Pancakes, 65
  Stroganoff, 101
  Trevarrick, 77
  Wellington, 13
Beefsteak and Cowheel Pie, 87
Beurre Manié: see Canard en Casserole, 18

Black Cherry and Rum Pie, 149
Blackberry and Apple Meringue, 87
Blackcurrant and Rum Parfait, 13
Boeuf à la Bourguignonne, 107
  Allumettes, 136
  en Chemise, 85
Bon Homme Canard, Normand, 118
Border Pasty, 141
Bourguignonne Apple Soup, 133
  Boeuf, 107
  Kidneys, 90
Braised Red Cabbage, Austrian, 63
Brandade, 55
Brandy Angel Mousse, 137
Breton Mussels, 87
Brimont Fonds d'Artichaut, 34
Bristol Noisettes de Veau, 35
Butter, Garlic, 104
  Walnut, 84
Butterscotch Pie, 57

Cabbage, Baked Spring, 149
  Braised Red, 63
Canard Bon Homme Normand, 118
  en Casserole aux Poivres Verts, 18
Cappucino Crêpes, 72
Caramel Meringue Glacé, 99
  Sauce, 152
Caramelised Peaches and Pears, 29
Carrot Cream Soup, 135
Cassis Pears, 55
Cassoulet de Castelnaudary, 69
Catalan Lamb, 59
Celery and Almond Soup, 51
Champignons Farcis Frits 'Gravetye', 63
Cheese and Ham Stuffing: see Champignons, 63
  and Onions, Lancashire, 147
  Profiteroles, 90
  Salad, 105
  Soup, 90
  Stuffing: see Priddy Oggy, 31
Cheesecake, Chocolate and Orange, 65
Chef's Terrine, 95
Cherry and Rum Pie, 149
  Batter: see Clafoutis Limousin, 52
Chestnut Cream, Pitt House, 27
  Turinois, 49
Cheval Blanc Prawns, 67

Chicken Dales Style, 123
  in Soya and Ginger Sauce, 28
  Jurasienne, 61
  Mexicana, 97
  Nanette, 43
  Soup: see Crème Marie Louise, 20
  Stock, 152
  Ulla, 55
  Véronique, 89
  with Apples and Cider, 144
  with Pernod, 80
Chilindron Lamb, 40
Chilled Cucumber Soup, 77
Chinese Orange Cake, 17
Chocolate and Orange Cheesecake, 65
  Mousse Harvey, 35
  Orange Mousse, 83
Choux Pastry: see Cheese Profiteroles, 90
Clafoutis Limousin, 52
Clams or Cockles with Pork, 103
  with Garlic Butter, 104
Clay-baked Venison, 141
Codling, Baked, 15
Cod's Roe and Smoked Salmon Paste, 103
Coffee and Almond Tart, 61
Cointreau Custard, 85
  Sauce, 109
Cold Leeks with Carrot, Tomato and Soured Cream, 149
Conserve, Orange, 32
Coquilles, Smoked Haddock, 78
Coulibiac, Salmon, 47
Cowheel and Beefsteak Pie, 87
Crab, Devilled, 26
  Stuffing: see Stuffed Aubergines, 48
Cream and Curry Sauce, 65, 83
  Cheese and Egg Mousse, 80
  Cheese Soup with Cheese Profiteroles, 90
  Cheese Taramasalata, 43
  Chestnut, 27
  Lemon Crumble, 18
  of Watercress Soup, 138
  Raspberry, 101
  Wiltshire, 37
Crème Brûlée, 41
  d'Or, 135
  Marie Louise, 20
  Pâtisserie, 79
Créole Bananas, 77

Crêpes, Batter for, 153
   Cappucino, 72
Crevettes en Quiche, 40
Croquettes, Stilton, 127
Croûtons, 153
Crumble Cream, Lemon, 18
Cucumber and Salmon Mousse, 142
   Fritters with Dill and Soured Cream, 45
   Ham and Mint Sauce, 17
   Sauce, 56
   Soup, Chilled, 77
Curd Tart, Yorkshire, 123
Curry Cream Sauce, 65, 83
Custard, Cointreau, 85

Dales Style Chicken, 123
Damson Soufflé, Iced, 89
Date and Herb Stuffing: see Gigot d'Agneau, 51
Deep-fried Mushrooms with Cucumber Sauce, 56
Devilled Crab, 26
Duck Casserole, 18
   Norman, 118
   Soup, 117
   Traditional Roast, 39
   with Cointreau Sauce, 109

Egg and Cream Cheese Mousse, 80
Escalope of Veal with Anchovy Sauce, 83
Espagnole Sauce, Quick, 152

Fegato alla Veneziana, 121
Ficelés Picards, 106
Filet de Boeuf en Chemise, 85
Fillet(s) of Beef Stroganoff, 101
   of Lemon Sole with Shrimp Sauce, 20
   of Pork, Barbecued, 49
   of Pork, Stuffed, 95
   of Pork with Apricots and Peppers, 75
Fish Soup, Norman, 118
   Stock, 152
Flambé Baked Alaska, 117
Fonds d'Artichaut Brimont, 34
Fool, Rhubarb, 43
Forcemeat: see Quail Pie, 104
Fresh Peach and Banana Pudding, 96
   Salmon and Cucumber Mousse, 142
Fried Rice, 49
Fritters, Aubergine, 28
   Cucumber, 45
Fudge and Walnut Pie, 81

Galette, Apple and Hazelnut, 91
Game Pie, Mr. Dupays', 24
Garlic Butter, 104

Garlic Croûtons, 153
   Mayonnaise: see Home-made Mayonnaise, 151
Gâteau Grison, 125
   Hazelnut Meringue, 143
Gigot d'Agneau Bédouin, 51
Ginger and Banana Meringue Cake, 15
   and Soya Sauce, 28
Globe Artichokes, 34
Gooseberry Sorbet, 45
Grand Marnier Soufflé, 112
Grapes in Cointreau Custard, 85
'Gravetye' Champignons Farcis Frits, 63
Greek Island Salad, 105
   Lemon Soup, 46
Green Pepper Stuffing, 143
Griesetorte, Lemon, 21
Grison Gâteau, 125
Guinea Fowl with Juniper Berries, 133

Haddock Coquilles, 78
   Mousse, 144
   Potted, 18
Ham and Cheese Stuffing: see Champignons, 63
   and Mushroom Stuffing: see Suprême de Volaille, 57
   Cucumber and Mint Sauce, 17
   Pancakes: see Ficelés Picards, 106
Hare, Jugged, 27
Harvey Chocolate Mousse, 35
Hazelnut and Apple Galette, 91
   Meringue Gâteau with Chocolate Sauce, 143
Herb and Date Stuffing: see Gigot d'Agneau, 51
   and Pork Stuffing: see Paupiettes de Veau, 111
   Forcemeat: see Quail Pie, 104
Hollandaise Sauce, 151
Homard Pool Court, 127
Homemade All-Purpose Stock, 152
   Mayonnaise, 151
   Tomato Sauce, 151
Hot Mousseline of Sole, 111
Hotpot, Mrs. Martin's Lancashire, 115

Iced Damson Soufflé, 89
   Orange Soufflé, 69

Jugged Hare, 27
Jurasienne Chicken, 61

Kidneys Bourguignonne, 90
Kipper(s) in Cream and Curry Sauce, 65
   Pâté, 101
Kitchen Garden Soup, 97

Lacock Liver Pâté, 39
Lamb, Bédouin, 51

Lamb Catalane, 59
   Chilindron, 40
   Leg, Stuffed with Apricots, 15
   Noisettes, 17
   Pilaff, Armenian, 71
   with Green Pepper Stuffing, 143
Lancashire Cheese and Onions, 147
   Hotpot, Mrs. Martin's, 115
Lancaster Lemon Tart, 115
Leeks, Cold, 149
Leg of Lamb Stuffed with Apricots, 15
Lemon Crumble Cream, 18
   Griesetorte, 21
   Posset, Marjorie's, 130
   Sole Fillets with Shrimp Sauce, 20
   Soup, Greek, 46
   Syllabub, 31
   Tart, Lancaster, 115
Limousin Clafoutis, 52
Liver Pâté, Lacock, 39
   Veneziana, 121
Lobster, Pool Court, 127
Loin of Lamb with Green Pepper Stuffing, 143

Malakoff Pudding, 75
Marie Louise Crème, 20
Marinaded Pork with Calvados, 128
Marjorie's Lemon Posset, 130
Mayonnaise, Homemade, 151
Meringue Baskets, Raspberry, 79
   Blackberry and Apple, 87
   Cake, Banana and Ginger, 15
   Gâteau, Hazelnut, 143
   Glacé, Caramel, 99
   Round for Pavlova, etc., 153
   with Pitt House Chestnut Cream, 27
Mexicana Chicken, 97
Mint, Cucumber and Ham Sauce, 17
   Orange and Recurrant Sauce, 143
Mousse, Brandy Angel, 137
   Chocolate Harvey, 35
   Chocolate Orange, 83
   Cream Cheese and Egg, 80
   Fresh Salmon and Cucumber, 142
   Orange, 150
   Sea Food, 12
   Smoked Haddock, 144
Mousseline of Sole, Hot, 111
   Salmon Trout, 75
Mr. Dupays' Game Pie, 24
Mrs. Martin's Lancashire Hotpot, 115
Mushroom and Ham Stuffing: see Suprême de Volaille, 57
   Armenian, 16

Mushrooms, Deep-fried, 56
  Stuffed, 63
Mussels Breton, 87
  to Clean, 153
Mutton Cassoulet, 69

Nanette Chicken, 43
Nettle Soup, 59
Nockerln, Salzburger, 63
Noisettes de Veau Bristol, 35
  of Lamb with Cucumber, Ham and Mint Sauce, 17
Norman Duck Bon Homme, 118
'Normandie' Soupe de Poisson, 118
Nut and Prune Stuffing: see Pork Fillet, 95

Oatmeal Parkin, Sticky, 147
Oggy, Priddy, 31
Old Rectory Snails, 121
Onion Wine Sauce: see Fegato, 121
Orange and Chocolate Cheesecake, 65
  Cake, Chinese, 17
  Chocolate Mousse, 83
  Conserve, 32
  Mousse, 150
  Redcurrant and Mint Sauce, 143
  Soufflé, Iced, 69

Pancake(s) Batter, 153
  Cappucino, 72
  Ham: see Ficelés Picards, 106
  Rare Beef, 65
Parfait à la Vanille, 107
  Rum and Blackcurrant, 13
Parkin, Sticky Oatmeal, 147
Pasty, Border, 141
Pâté, Kipper, 101
  Lacock Liver, 39
  Maison, 109
Pâtisserie Crème, 79
Paupiettes de Veau with Cucumbers, 111
Pavlova: see Meringue Round, 153
Peach(es) and Banana Pudding, 96
  and Pears, Caramelised, 29
  in Curry Cream Sauce, 83
Peanut Soup, 115
Pears and Peaches, Caramelised, 29
  in Cassis, 55
  Roquefort, 69
Peasant Soup, 141
Pepper Stuffing, 143
Pernod Chicken, 80
Petit Homard Pool Court, 127
Picardy Ficelés, 106
Pilaff, Armenian Lamb, 71

Piperade, 128
Pitt House Chestnut Cream, 27
Platte, Solothurner, 125
Poires au Roquefort, etc., 69
Poisson, 'Normandie' Soupe de, 118
Pool Court Lobster, 127
Porc à la Crème, 79
Pork Allumettes, 79
  and Herb Stuffing: see Paupiettes de Veau, 111
  and Tarragon Stuffing: see Chicken Jurasienne, 61
  Fillet, Barbecued, 49
  Fillet Stuffed with Walnuts, Prunes and Almonds, 95
  Fillet with Apricots and Peppers, 75
  in Pastry: see Priddy Oggy, 31
  Marinaded, 128
  with Clams or Cockles, 103
Port Wine Sauce, 67
Posset, Marjorie's Lemon, 130
Pot-roasted Rabbit in Port Wine Sauce, 67
Potted Haddock, 18
Prawn(s) Cheval Blanc, 67
  Quiche, 40
Priddy Oggy, 31
Priory Pudding, 25
Profiteroles, Cheese, 90
Prune and Nut Stuffing: see Pork Fillet, 95

Quail Pie with Forcemeat, 104
Quiche aux Crevettes, 40
Quick Espagnole Sauce, 152

Rabbit, Pot-roasted in Port Wine Sauce, 67
Rare Beef Pancakes, 65
Raspberry Cream, 101
  Meringue Baskets, 79
  Shortcake, 47
Red Cabbage, Austrian Braised, 63
  Wine Sauce: see Guinea Fowl, 133
Redcurrant, Orange and Mint Sauce, 143
Rhubarb Fool, 43
Rice, Fried, 49
Roast Duck, Traditional, 39
Roquefort Pears, 69
Rouille Sauce, 80
Roulage au Chinois, 134
Rum and Black Cherry Pie, 149
  and Blackcurrant Parfait, 13

Sage and Onion Stuffing, 39
Salad, Greek Island, 105
Salmon and Cod's Roe Paste, 103
  and Cucumber Mousse, 142
  Coulibiac, 47
  Soused, 37

Salmon Trout Mousseline, 75
Salzburger Nockerln, 63
Sauce(s), 151–2
  Anchovy, 83
  Apricot: see Fillet of Pork, 75
  Caramel, 152
  Cointreau, 109
  Cream and Curry, 65, 83
  Cucumber, 56
  Cucumber, Ham and Mint, 17
  Curry Cream, 65, 83
  Ginger and Soya, 28
  Hollandaise, 151
  Mayonnaise, 151
  Onion Wine, 121
  Orange, Redcurrant and Mint, 143
  Port Wine, 67
  Quick Espagnole, 152
  Red Wine: see Guinea Fowl, 133
  Rouille, 80
  Shrimp, 20
  Soured Cream: see Cucumber Fritters, 45
  Soya and Ginger, 28
  Tomato, 151
  Tomato and Tarragon, 28
  White Wine, 138
Schokoladentorte, Amaretti, 127
Scoblianka, 45
See Food Mousse, 12
Shortcake, Raspberry, 47
Shrimp Sauce, 20
Smoked Haddock Coquilles, 78
  Haddock Mousse, 144
  Salmon and Cod's Roe Paste, 103
Snails Old Rectory, 121
Sole au Vert-Pré, 60
  Lemon, 20
  Mousseline, Hot, 111
  St. Germain, 23
Solothurner Platte, 125
Sorbet, Gooseberry, 45
Soufflé, Grand Marnier, 112
  Iced Damson, 89
  Iced Orange, 69
Soupe de Poisson 'Normandie', 118
Soured Cream Sauce: see Cucumber Fritters, 45
Soused Salmon, 37
Soya and Ginger Sauce, 28
Spotted Dick with Syrup Sauce, 145
Spring Cabbage Baked in Oil and Garlic with Juniper
  Berries, 149
St. Germain Sole, 23
Steak Solothurner, 125
  Sussex, 37

Sticky Oatmeal Parkin, 147
Stilton Croquettes, 127
    Pears, 69
Stocks, 152
Stroganoff Beef Fillet, 101
Stuffed Aubergines, 48
    Mushrooms, 63
    Pork Fillet, 95
Stuffing, Apricot: see Leg of Lamb, 15
    Cheese: see Priddy Oggy, 31
    Cheese and Ham: see Champignons, 63
    Crab: see Stuffed Aubergines, 48
    Date and Herb: see Gigot d'Agneau, 51
    Forcemeat: see Quail Pie, 104
    Green Pepper, 143
    Ham and Mushroom: see Suprême de Volaille, 57
    Pork and Herb: see Paupiettes de Veau, 111
    Pork and Tarragon: see Chicken Jurasienne, 61
    Prune and Nut: see Pork Fillet, 95
    Sage and Onion, 39
    Tarragon: see Quail Pie, 104
Suprêmes de Volaille Farcie, 57

Sussex Steak, 37
Sweetbreads in Cream and White Wine, 138
Syllabub, Lemon, 31

Taramasalata, 71
    with Cream Cheese, 43
Tarragon and Pork Stuffing: see Chicken Jurasienne, 61
    and Tomato Sauce, 28
    Stuffing: see Quail Pie, 104
Terrine du Chef, 95
Tipsy Cake, 109
Tomato and Tarragon Sauce, 28
    Sauce, 151: see also Marinaded Pork, 128
Traditional Roast Duck with Sage and Onion, 39
Tranche d'Agneau à la Catalane, 59
Trevarrick Beef, 77
Trout Mousseline, Salmon, 75
Turinois Chestnut, 49

Ulla Chicken, 55

Vanilla Parfait, 107

Veal Escalope with Anchovy Sauce, 83
    Noisettes Bristol, 35
    Paupiettes with Cucumbers, 111
    Scoblianka, 45
Venison Cooked in Clay, 141
Venetian Liver, 121
Véronique Chicken, 89
Vert-Pré Sole, 60
Volaille Farcie, Suprême de, 57

Walnut and Fudge Pie, 81
    Butter, 84
Watercress Cream Soup, 138
Wellington Beef, 13
White Wine Sauce, 138
Wiltshire Cream, 37
Wine Onion Sauce: see Fegato, 121

Yeast Pastry: see Salmon Coulibiac, 47
Yorkshire Curd Tart, 123

Zabaglione, 121

157

Classified Index

Appetisers or Starters

Armenian Mushrooms, 16
Aubergine Fritters with Tomato and Tarragon Sauce, 28

Baked Avocado with Walnut Butter, 84
Brandade, 55

Champignons Farcis Frits 'Gravetye', 63
Clams with Garlic Butter, 104
Cold Leeks with Carrot, Tomato and Soured Cream, 149
Cream Cheese and Egg Mousse, 80
Cucumber Fritters with Dill and Soured Cream, 45

Deep-fried Mushrooms with Cucumber Sauce, 56
Devilled Crab, 26

Ficelés Picards, 106
Fonds d'Artichaut Brimont, 34
Fresh Salmon and Cucumber Mousse, 142

Greek Island Salad, 105

Hot Mousseline of Sole, 111

Kipper(s) in Cream and Curry Sauce, 65
   Pâté, 101

Lacock Liver Pâté, 39
Lancashire Cheese and Onions, 147

Mussels Breton, 87

Pâté Maison, 109
Peaches in Curry Cream Sauce, 83
Piperade, 128
Poires au Roquefort, etc., 69
Potted Haddock, 18
Prawns Cheval Blanc, 67

Quiche aux Crevettes, 40

Salmon Trout Mousseline, 75
Sea Food Mousse, 12
Smoked Haddock Coquilles, 78
   Haddock Mousse, 144
   Salmon and Cod's Roe Paste, 103
Snails Old Rectory, 121
Sole St. Germain, 23
Soused Salmon, 37
Stilton Croquettes, 127
Stuffed Aubergines, 48

Taramasalata, 71
   with Cream Cheese, 43
Terrine du Chef, 95

Soups, Stocks

All-Purpose Stock, 152
Apple Soup à la Bourguignonne, 133
Avgolemono, 46

Celery and Almond Soup, 51
Chicken Stock, 152
Chilled Cucumber Soup, 77
Cream Cheese Soup with Cheese Profiteroles, 90
   of Watercress Soup, 138
Crème d'Or, 135
   Marie Louise, 20

Duck Soup, 117

Fish Stock, 152

Kitchen Garden Soup, 97

Nettle Soup, 59
'Normandie' Soupe de Poisson, 118

Peanut Soup, 115
Pheasant Soup, 141

Fish, Shellfish

Baked Codling, 15
Brandade, 55

Clams with Garlic Butter, 104

Devilled Crab, 26

Fillets of Lemon Sole with
   Shrimp Sauce, 20
Fish Stock, 152
Fresh Salmon and Cucumber
   Mousse, 142

Hot Mousseline of Sole, 111

Kipper(s) in Cream and Curry
   Sauce, 65
   Pâté, 101

Lemon Sole, 20

Mussels Breton, 87
   to Clean, 153

'Normandie' Soupe de Poisson, 118

Petit Homard Pool Court, 127
Potted Haddock, 18
Prawns Cheval Blanc, 67

Quiche aux Crevettes, 40

Salmon Coulibiac, 47
   Trout Mousseline, 75
Sea Food Mousse, 12
Smoked Haddock Coquilles, 78
   Haddock Mousse, 144
   Salmon and Cod's Roe Paste, 103
Sole au Vert-Pré, 60
   St. Germain, 23
Soused Salmon, 37

Taramasalata, 71
   with Cream Cheese, 43

Meat

Allumettes de Boeuf, 136
   de Porc à la Crème, 79
Armenian Lamb Pilaff, 71

Barbecued Pork Fillet with Fried Rice, 49
Beef and Red Wine Pie, 147
   Trevarrick, 77
   Wellington, 13
Beefsteak and Cowheel Pie, 87
Boeuf à la Bourguignonne, 107

Cassoulet de Castelnaudary, 69

Escalope of Veal with Anchovy Sauce, 83

Fegato alla Veneziana, 121
Filet de Boeuf en Chemise, 85
Fillet of Beef Stroganoff, 101
   of Pork with Apricots and Peppers, 75

Gigot d'Agneau Bédouin, 51

Kidneys Bourguignonne, 90

Lacock Liver Pâté, 39
Lamb Chilindron, 40
Leg of Lamb Stuffed with Apricots, 15
Loin of Lamb with Green Pepper Stuffing, 143

Marinaded Pork with Calvados, 128
Mrs. Martin's Lancashire Hotpot, 115

Noisettes de Veau Bristol, 35
   of Lamb with Cucumber, Ham and Mint Sauce, 17

Pâté Maison, 109
Paupiettes de Veau with Cucumber, 111

Pork Fillet Stuffed with Walnuts, Prunes and Almonds, 95
  with Clams or Cockles, 103
Pot-roasted Rabbit in Port Wine Sauce, 67
Priddy Oggy, 31

Rare Beef Pancakes, 65

Scoblianka, 45
Solothurner Platte, 125
Sussex Steak, 37
Sweetbreads in Cream and White Wine, 138

Terrine du Chef, 95
Tranche d'Agneau à la Catalane, 59

Poultry, Game

Canard Bon Homme Normand, 118
  en Casserole aux Poivres Verts, 18
Chicken Dales Style, 123
  in Soya and Ginger Sauce, 28
  Jurasienne, 61
  Mexicana, 97
  Nanette, 43
  Soup: see Crème Marie Louise, 20
  Ulla, 55
  Véronique, 89
  with Apples and Cider, 144
  with Pernod, 80

Duck with Cointreau Sauce, 109

Guinea Fowl with Juniper Berries, 133

Jugged Hare, 27

Mr. Dupays' Game Pie, 24

Quail Pie with Forcemeat, 104

Roast Duck with Sage and Onion, 39

Suprême de Volaille Farcie, 57

Venison Cooked in Clay, 141

Cheese, Eggs

Cream Cheese and Egg Mousse, 80
  Cheese Soup with Cheese
    Profiteroles, 90

Greek Island Salad, 105

Lancashire Cheese and Onions, 147

Poires au Roquefort (or Stilton), 69

Stilton Croquettes, 127

Taramasalata with Cream Cheese, 143

Salad, Vegetables, etc.

Armenian Mushrooms, 16
Aubergine Fritters with Tomato
  and Tarragon Sauce, 28
Austrian Braised Red Cabbage, 63

Baked Avocado with Walnut Butter, 84

Champignons Farcis Frits 'Gravetye', 63
Cold Leeks with Carrot, Tomato and
  Soured Cream, 149
Cucumber Fritters with Dill and
  Soured Cream, 45

Deep-fried Mushrooms with Cucumber Sauce, 56

Fonds d'Artichaut Brimont, 34
Fried Rice, 49

Greek Island Salad, 105

Pilaff Rice, 71
Piperade, 128

Spring Cabbage Baked in Oil and Garlic
  with Juniper Berries, 149
Stuffed Aubergines, 48

Sauces

Anchovy, 83
Apricot: see Fillet of Pork, 75

Caramel, 152
Cointreau, 109
Cream and Curry, 65, 83
Cucumber, 56
  Ham and Mint, 17

Hollandaise, 151

Mayonnaise, 151

Onion Wine: see Fegato, 121
Orange, Redcurrant and Mint, 143

Port Wine, 67

Quick Espagnole, 152

Red Wine: see Guinea Fowl, 133
Rouille, 80

Shrimp, 20
Soured Cream: see Cucumber Fritters, 45

Soya and Ginger, 28

Tomato, 151: see also Marinaded Pork, 128
  and Tarragon, 28

White Wine, 138

Stuffings, Forcemeat

Apricot: see Leg of Lamb, 15

Cheese: see Priddy Oggy, 31
  and Ham: see Champignons, 63
Crab: see Stuffed Aubergines, 48

Date and Herb: see Gigot d'Agneau, 51

Forcemeat: see Quail Pie, 104

Green Pepper, 143

Ham and Mushroom: see Suprême de Volaille, 57

Pork and Herb: see Paupiettes de Veau, 111
  and Tarragon: see Chicken Jurasienne, 61
Prune and Nuts: see Pork Fillet, 95

Sage and Onion, 39

Tarragon: see Quail Pie, 104

Sweet Course, Cakes

Amaretti Schokoladentorte, 127
Apple and Almond Pudding, 39
  and Hazelnut Galette, 91

Baked Alaska Flambé, 117
Banana and Ginger Meringue Cake, 15
  Créole, 77
Blackberry and Apple Meringue, 87
Border Pasty, 141
Butterscotch Pie, 57

Caramel Meringue Glacé, 99
Caramelised Peaches and Pears, 29
Chestnut Turinois, 49
Chinese Orange Cake, 17
Chocolate and Orange Cheesecake, 65
  Mousse Harvey, 35
  Orange Mousse, 83
Clafoutis Limousin, 52
Coffee and Almond Tart, 61
Crème Brûlée, 41
Crêpes: see Batter, 153
  Cappucino, 72

Fresh Peach and Banana Pudding, 96
Fudge and Walnut Pie, 81

159

Gâteau Grison, 125
Gooseberry Sorbet, 45
Grapes in Cointreau Custard, 85

Hazelnut Meringue Gâteau with Chocolate Sauce, 143

Iced Damson Soufflé, 89
  Orange Soufflé, 69

Lancaster Lemon Tart, 115
Lemon Crumble Cream, 18
  Griesetorte, 21
  Syllabub, 31

Malakoff Pudding, 75
Marjorie's Lemon Posset, 130

Meringue with Pitt House Chestnut Cream, 27

Orange Conserve, 32
  Mousse, 150

Pancakes: see Batter, 153
Parfait à la Vanille, 107
Pavlova: see Meringue Round, 153
Pears in Cassis, 55
Priory Pudding, 25

Raspberry Cream, 101
  Meringue Baskets, 79
  Shortcake, 47
Rhubarb Fool, 43

Roulage au Chinois, 134
Rum and Black Cherry Pie, 149
  and Blackcurrant Parfait, 13

Salzburger Nockerln, 63
Soufflé Grand Marnier, 112
Spotted Dick with Syrup Sauce, 145
Sticky Oatmeal Parkin, 147

Tipsy Cake, 109

Wiltshire Cream, 37

Yorkshire Curd Tart, 123

Zabaglione, 121